From Teaching to Coaching your TEEN
A pathway for parents to connect and raise confident teenagers who are mentally strong and sound.

From Teaching to Coaching your TEEN

A pathway for parents to connect and raise confident teenagers who are mentally strong and sound.

Nene C. Oluwagbohun

Foreword by Jane Onuh Eben-Spiff
B.Sc Psych, M.A. HRM

XULON PRESS

Xulon Press
2301 Lucien Way #415
Maitland, FL 32751
407.339.4217
www.xulonpress.com

© 2022 by Nene C. Oluwagbohun

All rights reserved solely by the author. The author guarantees all contents are original and do not infringe upon the legal rights of any other person or work. No part of this book may be reproduced in any form without the permission of the author.

Due to the changing nature of the Internet, if there are any web addresses, links, or URLs included in this manuscript, these may have been altered and may no longer be accessible. The views and opinions shared in this book belong solely to the author and do not necessarily reflect those of the publisher. The publisher therefore disclaims responsibility for the views or opinions expressed within the work.

Unless otherwise indicated, Scripture quotations taken from the King James Version (KJV) – *public domain.*

Scripture quotations taken from the Holy Bible, New International Version (NIV). Copyright © 1973, 1978, 1984, 2011 by Biblica, Inc.™. Used by permission. All rights reserved.

Scripture quotations taken from The Message (MSG). Copyright © 1993, 1994, 1995, 1996, 2000, 2001, 2002. Used by permission of NavPress Publishing Group. Used by permission. All rights reserved.

Scripture taken from The Passion Translation (TPT). Copyright © 2017 by Passion & Fire Ministries, Inc. Used by permission. All rights reserved. thePassionTranslation.com

Paperback ISBN-13: 978-1-6628-6510-7
Ebook ISBN-13: 978-1-6628-6511-4

Table of Contents

CHAPTER 1
Don't Parent by Assumption   1

CHAPTER 2
Acquiring Knowledge   12

CHAPTER 3
Who Is a Teacher?   16

CHAPTER 4
Every Child Desires a Teacher   27

CHAPTER 5
Teach Spiritual Matter   35

CHAPTER 6
Teach Values of Life   57

CHAPTER 7
Teach Soft Skills   68

CHAPTER 8
Be a Great Friend   86

CHAPTER 9
Instructing   92

CHAPTER 10
Coaching   108

Foreword

Raising teenagers can seem daunting, however your ability to stay the course and keep learning along the pathway, makes the difference in successful parenting.

This book is packed with insight that will illuminate your understanding of your teenager, what do they really need? How can they thrive in a world full of peer pressure and misinformation? Why are conversations heated? How do I communicate more effectively? How can I support my child to keep a healthy mindset and enable them set healthy boundaries when it is required?

This book shares practical advice that answers these questions and points you towards partnership with God as you raise your teenager. The writer steps right into your home and holds your hand through this book until you regain balance in your journey.

I recommend this book not only to parents of teens, but also to parents who are preparing for their children in advance of becoming teens, teachers who work with teens, coaches, and grandparents.

The chapters come alive as you read, exhorting you while reaffirming your innate superior ability to guide your teenager into oneness with God, Family and Self.

Enjoy this book, practice its revelations, and become that catalyst to coach your teen into their God given purpose and destiny!

Jane Onuh Eben-Spiff
B.Sc Psych, M.A. HRM

Introduction

Being a parent is one of the most difficult and challenging responsibilities anyone would ever face because children do not come with a specificity manual. Children grow into adults, and if you have been relating with human beings for a while on earth as an adult, you will agree with me that they could be the most difficult creatures on earth. As parents, God has given us the responsibility to parent His 'heritage,' and 'precious possession'–children. Psalm 127:3 (NKJV) which says, *"Children are a heritage from the Lord."* A heritage is something of esteemed value to someone, something important, that needs to be bequeaths to a loved ones. This means children are immensely valuable to God. If you are a parent, you have been entrusted with a child and given the opportunity to nurture them into adulthood. What a great privilege and high calling!

Knowing children do not come with a specificity parenting manual; it's no wonder we ache for answers because of our feelings of inadequacy, even after we try to educate ourselves through parenting books and seminars, there are inadequacies that stem from the fragmented and strained relationships that comes with parenting.

What if, through this book I again suggest one more try?

I agree that we do not have a manual for the little, tiny creatures sent to us to nurture, but we can personally get connected to the one who made them and knitted them together in our wombs. David in Psalm 139:13 (NIV) said, *"For you created my inmost being; you knit me together in my mother's womb."* In Jeremiah 1:5 (NIV) God Himself states this: *"Before I formed you in the womb I knew you, before you were born, I set you apart; I appointed you as a prophet to the nations."* And again, He said in Jeremiah 29:11 (NIV), *"For I know the plans I have for you,"* declares the Lord, *"plans to prosper you and not to harm you, plans to give you hope and a future."*

So if God knitted that tiny little baby together in your womb, it means he knew them before they were even put in your womb. If he declared He had a set plan for them, then I think its best we partnered with Him because He would definitely have the manual and the template we are looking for.

Doesn't this fix the puzzle?

God has the template!

If the one who created children has the manual and template, isn't it best to partner with, and follow Him?

In our parenting journey, the template we follow could leave an indelible positive legacy in our wake. It can also ensure that our children are kept and connected to God even after we are gone. Keep in mind that the template you follow has the capacity to impact and influence generations after you, to your third and fourth generations. It is then pertinent to be intentional about the model you want to use.

Every child is unique and special. The one who created them can best show you how to connect to them if you let him guide you.

Now, let's look at his templates. One of His major templates comes as an instruction in Proverbs 22:6 (KJV), it says: *"Train up a child in the way he should go: and when he is old, he will not depart from it."* The word *train* here involves teaching, instructing, and coaching. Every child comes blank, deeply desiring a teacher, an instructor, and a coach in their life's journey. Stepping up to doing the job of a teacher, an instructor and coach builds a long-lasting relationship with your child.

In Deuteronomy 6:7 (NKJV), God laid down one of the templates for parenting, called teaching. The verse instructs, *"And thou shalt teach them diligently unto thy children."* The word *diligently* here means **to do something continually, tirelessly, deliberately, and intentionally**. This process of parenting can be very tedious; it requires a lot of time, emotions, energy, and resources. It is definitely a process we cannot miss out on if we wish to see tangible results. This process also requires a lot of planning, knowledge, precision, and decisiveness. Consequently, we must partner with God to gain the wisdom that will enable us navigate the processes and stages of development our children must go through smoothly. We must also remember to meet their emotional, mental, and spiritual needs by staying connected to them through every stage of growth.

It Is Teaching—Instructing—Coaching

The Process of Building a Team

No good player joins a new team assuming.
A child signs up for a game.
He is first taught about the game, the
rules of the game and his position.
He is placed in the game to play with an expectation
to follow instructions the coach gives;
Then he is placed in the field to play independently. He must
then listen for the coach's voice to play the game competently.

Nene C. Oji-okoro Oluwagbohun

Organization
Employ—teach—deploy—coach

Jesus
Calls them—Teaches them—Instructs them to go and teach others, and He sent the Holy Spirit to coach.

Church
Born again—Teach—Deploy and Coach

Parenting
Teach—Instruct—Coach

CHAPTER 1

Don't Parent by Assumption

"No good player joins a new team assuming."
—Nene Oluwagbohun

"Most of our assumptions have outlived their uselessness."
—Marshall McLuhan[1]

"A fool takes no pleasure in understanding, but only in expressing his opinion."
—Proverbs 18:2 (ESV)

What Is Assumption?

The *Britannica Dictionary*' definition of ASSUMPTION is, "something that is believed to be true but is not known to be true." As parents, it is very unhealthy to assume when it comes to raising children.

Our beliefs can impact how we see and understand things daily, and if these beliefs are not true, their lie will then limit our potential and of those around us. The truth is, the more we believe something to be true, the more they appear true, even if they are in the real sense untrue. This is what assumptions can do in our lives. We must steer clear of the many assumptions we have so we don't carry them into parenting. It will be sad to see it negatively impact our duties and relationship with the children.

To mention a few, here are some assumptions parents run with:

There are no templates for raising children:

I will like to say man-made templates for raising children are assumptions and not the truth if they do not follow **the template laid out by God.** In Proverbs 22:6 (NKJV) He said, *"Train up a child in the way he should go: and when he is old, he will not depart from it."* This is a template. Imbedded in this template is an instruction that categorically states how we should raise our children- The word *train* is the operative word.

Imbedded in the word *train* is; **teach, instruct,** and **coach**. It is a process of impacting someone with new knowledge and skill. Quite frankly, if we want to see lasting results in our children's lives, 'training' them has to be a conscious, consistent and intentional effort. It's beyond academics or going to church; it is not merely having collaborations and support from other people, the parent must be personally involved in training their child.

When we become deliberate to follow this template that says; "train," we will raise healthy, strong, wise, and wholesome children. Your presence and your involvement in the training of your children will leave a lasting bound and connection between you and your child. Wouldn't you like that?

You are not fit or qualified to be a parent:

This may seem true because of your inadequacies but you are enough. When God looks at you, He sees one who is worthy of His gift and wants you to seek Him so He can show you how to be a great parent. Psalm 127:3 (NIV) reiterates this, it says; "Children are a heritage from the LORD, offspring a reward from him." According to the Oxford Dictionary, the word **heritage** means a property that is or may be inherited, or a valued object. This implies that children are God's valuable and precious property handed over to you to nurture. You do not own the children; they belong to God. If He didn't trust you, He wouldn't entrust you with His **heritage.**

God saw that you were capable and able, so He sent that child to you to nurture for him. In John 15:16 (NIV) He tells us: *"You did not choose me, but I chose you and appointed you so that you might go and bear fruit—fruit that will last."* Know this: you were chosen and appointed by the Maker of heaven and earth Himself to serve Him in this capacity of parenting His **heritage.**

You are qualified; you are fit and graced to do it. How cool is that?

Stop listening to the voice of doubt. You are an amazing parent; God Himself handpicked you. He knows you can. Stop worrying and partner with the One who finds you worthy of the honor of raising His **Heritage.** Ask Him to help you for He is a willing and capable partner. Open your heart and acknowledge that you are everything He sees in you. Take up this parenting assignment and do it. God's got you!

Children are terrible in their twos:

Children are like seeds. When you plant a seed, you are expected to nurture it to grow well. Bear in mind that parenting is the act of nurturing the seed, called children to grow well. One effective tool for nurturing these seeds are words. Like we say in Africa, "Words have power." Proverbs 18:21(NIV) also attests to this. It tells us that, *"Life and death are in the power of the tongue."* You see, calling them **terrible twos** means they are not good seeds. It means you are speaking negative words into them. They are not **terrible**; their behavior at that age is usually **a cry for help, indicating that something needs to be fixed**. This is Reminiscent of the farmer, who notices the seed being attacked by pests because it is growing poorly. He does not call the seed he has planted terrible, but addresses the attacker of the seed by getting rid of the pests, nurturing the seed or plant back to good health.

Children are built the same.

When they misbehavior, it simply means they need some more nurturing. Instead of labeling them, it is your job to pull out the harmful weeds by correcting them and teaching them. Proverbs 22:15 (NIV) says, *"Foolishness is bound in the heart of a child, but the rod of correction will drive it out."* Notice that it did not say the child is foolish; it said the problem is in the heart, meaning something is attacking the heart, that is why the child is acting foolishly. Foolishness here means, lack of good sense. They child lacks knowledge of what to do, or what is good or bad, The *rod* of correction, here at this stage, means that words (teaching), attention, and nurturing will drive what is attacking the child's heart away. It's all part of training.

Parenting a teenager is miserable:

This is an assumption many parents run with when their children are becoming teenagers. People have a lot of negative expectations for this period. Mainly because at this stage, teenagers are finding themselves, grappling with hormonal and biological changes happening in their body resulting to mood swings, unpredictable or irrational behaviors. Folks must learn to approach this period without anxiety, trepidation and judgment.

The best thing a parent can do is prepare for this stage. Be ready hold deep conversation, support and empathize with them. It is a phase that must pass. The teenagers simply need parental support to manage the chemical transformations and changes in their bodies.

Let's not approach the teenage phase being judgmental because children can perceive the silent criticism. They will smell the apprehension and fear, which may then give the devil room to manipulate the situation for them to manifest your fears . Matthew 7:1 (NIV) says it all: *"Judge not, that ye be not judged."* When we approach our children in a less judgmental way, they become more open and willing to come to us for help.

In the first place, God never called them teenagers; that is a label by the system of this world. In Acts 2:17 and Joel 2:28, the Bible calls them "your young" [who] will see vision. Our young men and women will see visions, and they will be called blessed as we teach them.

There are many young men and women in the Bible who did great things as teenagers because they were taught. There's Daniel and his friends in Babylon, David killed Goliath as a teenager, Esther became a queen and saved her people as a teenager, many of Jesus's disciples were teenagers, and after them came Timothy in the Bible, who served God as a teenager.

Parenting a teenager is an amazing thing to do. At this stage, our young children are experiencing life in its practical ways. They are learning the ropes of being independent, being decisive about their choices and being responsible. Your support and encouragement empowers them with courage to become better.

When you empathize with them, it takes out the bite of judgment. Asking open-ended questions with an open heart, genuinely intending to hear their thoughts shows them that you have chosen to believe and see the good and kind, as well as hear that which is of good report about them according to Philippians 4:8 (NLT). This verse says, *"And now, dear brothers and sisters, one final thing. Fix your thoughts on what is true, and honorable, and right, and pure, and lovely, and admirable. Think about things that are excellent and worthy of praise."* If you do exactly as this verse admonishes, you will be surprised at how they will take responsibility for their actions while you coach them to navigate this stage. (We will talk about this in details in a future chapter).

Training a child is the job of the mother: No, dear parent, training children is the job of both parents, not the job of the mother, I totally understand it's a social norm, but we must understand that each parent has a role to play in the life of their child. You are a team put together to carry out this assignment, each playing their unique part. Let's look at Samson's parents, who raised their child as a team. Judges 13:8 (NKJV) tells us, *"Then Manoah prayed to the LORD: "Pardon your servant, Lord. I beg you to let the man of God you sent to US come again to TEACH US how to bring up the boy who is to be born."* They didn't only admit they needed to do it together, they also acknowledged they needed to be taught so they could raise the boy well.

You are a team, and team members always have a common goal and a leader. In the case of parenting, God is the leader.

The Lord has promised us His unflinching support as we carry one His assignment. A threefold cord is what your family should be. According to Ecclesiastes 4:12 (NKJV); *"Though one may be overpowered by another, two can withstand him. And a threefold cord is not quickly broken."* If we acknowledge Him, He will always be there to lead and support us, as we allow Him to be part of our home and parenting system if we let Him.

A threefold parenting cord, which is (God, father, and mother), will always be victorious and strong.

Our children will know about our God in church or at the temple:

The home was first designed before other systems. Our children should know about God from us, at home. God is pleased when parents teach their children about Him. God said of His friend Abraham in Genesis 18:19 (KJV): *"For I know him, that he will command his children and his household after him, and they shall keep the way of the LORD, to do justice and judgment."* He also commands us to teach and impress His Word in the hearts and minds of our children.

Deuteronomy 6:6–7, (NKJV) tells us, *"These commandments that I give you today are to be on your hearts. Impress them on your children. Talk about them when you sit at home and when you walk along the road, when you lie down and when you get up."*

From our reading here, we see that God did not say the church or school is responsible to teach our children; rather, we see that it is the responsibility of the parent. The church and school are designed to be support systems. God has set the template to start from home, and if you have not set that template, don't go demanding for it from your church or school.

We assume our children are too young to understand God:

This is a very interesting assumption, because we teach our children things they have never seen before nor eaten before, and they understand. They watch cartons, they watch us act and speak, they in turn understand most of it to role-play and imitate us. What makes you think they will not understand anything about God? We forget that our children existed in His presence before they were sent to the earth. Jeremiah 1:5(NIV) *"Before I formed you in the womb I knew you, before you were born I set you apart."* God is saying here, your child existed in the spirit before he was deployed to wear this human body here on earth. Your child is a spirit, wearing an earthly garment called his or her body. When they die, they will leave this earthly garment (their body) and their spirit will return to their original Father called *God* because He is the Father of all spirits- See, Hebrews 12:9 (NIV) which declares; *"How much more should we submit to the Father of spirits and live!"*

We are just earthly parents, bound by time to take care of them here on earth. Your child's original Father is God. He is timeless, and they will be with Him forever as spirits when their time on earth is done and their assignments are over, they will return to Him, not you to remain timeless, just as He is. Every child wants to hear about God. They know Him more than you think.

They are sent here on earth with a purpose and on an assignment because everything God has created is for a purpose (Prov. 16:4 NIV). To achieve that purpose and assignment, they need to stay connected to their heavenly Father, and parents are responsible for creating that atmosphere where they can stay connected to God.

It is important they stay connected to Him because fulfilling their purpose on earth successfully is dependent on their relationship with God. Keep talking to them about God; they are not too young to know God, and don't worry about how they will understand. The Holy Spirit will do the rest because they are spiritual beings, and it is a spiritual matter.

Now, if you do not know how to start off this parenting template, you can learn. Learning is a continuous process, and the Holy Spirit is here to help and support you. In parenting, it is very dangerous to make assumptions, even though we all do. Be that as it may, it's too risky to continue to dwell in assumptions because it can affect us in the long run. Instead of assuming, I suggest you ask questions and seek knowledge. Knowledge is very powerful. It can set you free, light your path, and empower you and your children yet unborn.

Here are a few dangers of assuming:

a. Assumptions limit people.
b. Assumptions make one judgmental which causes one to draw wrong conclusions.
c. Assumptions promote the transfer of wrong information.
d. Assumptions can be very destructive, breaking relationships, trust, and loyalty.
e. Assumptions lead to a primitive lifestyle.
f. Assumptions move us away from the truth.

Proverbs 18:2 (ESV) refers to one who lives on assumption as a fool. It is wiser to stop assuming and begin to acquire knowledge and understanding to help you step into your role of a teacher so you can equip your children and train them to be outstanding young men and women.

CHAPTER 2

Acquiring Knowledge

"Live as if you were to die tomorrow. Learn as if you were to live forever."
—Mahatma Gandhi[2]

"In learning you will teach, and in teaching you will learn."
—Phil Collins[3]

"The heart of the prudent getteth knowledge; and the ear of the wise seeketh knowledge."
—Proverbs 18:15 (KJV)

The Bible encourages us in 2 Timothy 2:15 (KJV): *"Study to shew ourselves approved unto God, a workman that needed not to be ashamed, rightly dividing the word of truth."* This means the lack of knowledge could lead to shame and destruction. I always say information is golden, and learning is a process, it's time to seek for knowledge. The Oxford Dictionary says learning means to acquire knowledge. Hosea 4:6 (KJV) reveals the danger of refusing to acquire knowledge: *"My people are destroyed for lack of knowledge: because thou hast rejected knowledge, I will also reject thee, that thou shalt be no priest to me: seeing thou hast forgotten the law of thy God, I will also forget thy children."*

Here we see that our rejection of knowledge could lead to God rejecting us; this is serious. The reason most people fail in what they do, even parenting, is because they fail to acquire knowledge. In that same verse, we read through Hosea where our rejection of knowledge could go as far as affecting our children. Hence, it is important for us to get knowledge so we can be empowered to carry out our parenting assignment effectively and efficiently.

Parenting can be learned. While parenting comes to others by nature, for some, they have to actively learn to avoid raising children in assumptions. The Bible in Proverbs 1:5 (NKJV) tells us that; *"A wise man will hear and increase learning; and a man of understanding shall attain unto wise counsel."* This means that it is wisdom to keep learning and acquiring knowledge.

One can acquire knowledge by going for trainings and investing in books. There are many benefits of educating yourself and your spouse in preparation for the arrival of your child or even at different stages of your children's growth and development.

Each stage of a child's development comes with its unique characteristics, challenges, and joys. It is a great opportunity for one to prepare and become more aware to escape avoidable mistakes from occurring. Acquiring parenting knowledge aids positive and best parenting practices for creating a healthy psychological, emotional, mental, and spiritual environment for everyone, which invariably makes our communities better too.

Getting parenting knowledge brings clarity to the roles and responsibilities of parenting for the parents. This then empowers them with the tools and strategies needed to nurture each child appropriately to thrive in life.

Children raised where positive and strategic parenting practices were deployed have been said to have developed highly emotionally, intellectually, spiritually, and socially. They are said to be more focused, self-aware, and appropriately behaved because their parents were clear on their roles and responsibilities and consciously built connections with their children.

Learning the art of parenting has lots of benefits for you, your child, and the society at large. Here are some benefits:

- It will eradicate lots of fears and assumptions that could lead to lots of parenting errors.
- Learning the art of parenting will enhance your mental wellbeing.
- Learning the art of parenting will reduce anxiety, anger, guilt, and stress that come with the confusion of raising children at different stages.

- Learning the art of parenting will improve your communication style with your children, you will be better prepared for the different stages of their growth, and you understand how to engage more.
- Learning the art of parenting would empower your leadership position in your home.
- Learning the art of parenting reduces the possibility of child abuse in the home as parents learn appropriate ways to discipline.
- Learning the art of parenting helps parent build healthy family culture and traditions that enhance love in the family.
- Learning the art of parenting helps parents understand ways to bond with their children and achieve their family goals and vision together.

As we learn, we are empowered to grow, teach, and lead. We become willing teachers who partner with the institution of heaven, recognizing and acknowledging all heaven sees in a child when others don't. We become teachers who, reliant on the Holy Spirit for help, ready to impact and empower the child to take on the assignments they have been deployed to carry out here on earth.

"Leadership and learning are indispensable to each other."
—John F. Kennedy[4]

CHAPTER 3

Who Is a Teacher?

"Every first-time player is taught the game, the rule of the game and their position by a teacher."
—Nene Oluwagbohun

"Teaching is a calling too. And I've always thought that teachers in their way are holy angels leading their flocks out of darkness."
—Jeannette Walls[5]

"Therefore, an overseer must be above reproach, the husband of one wife, sober-minded, self-controlled, respectable, hospitable, **able to teach**.*"*
—1 Timothy 3:2 (ESV)

A teacher is one who explains and demonstrates the right way of doing things. They empower others with knowledge, inspiring and equipping them to become great in life. Teaching is not just a formal thing done in schools or as a career; it is a mandate from God that must be carried out in every home. It is the first template of parenting commanded

by God in Deuteronomy 6:7. Here, God commands that; "...
thou shalt teach them."

Teaching is the greatest gift we can give our children. Teaching builds, impacts, empowers and makes our children become effective adults who make our world a better place. The moment a child is born, a parent becomes a teacher, teaching the child from an early age with the use of age-appropriate language. This starts *before* they are three or four years old, at the time children engage more by asking questions. This is the time they are curious about why and how things are done. This is a great time to dive in and teach your child.

Engaging with our children at this age is the starting point for building a wealth of knowledge before they begin going to formal school. This is when to establish that you are their first teacher. If you utilize this time effectively, you can build a long-lasting impact and deepen your connection with them to last through childhood to adulthood.

Teaching is a long-lasting calling that has great benefits in your life and that of your children. Someone once asked me; ***"who is a teacher?"*** Here is how I responded:

T—Truthful
E—Empathetic
A—Authentic
C—Caring
H—Helpful
E—Encouraging
R—Role Model

A Teacher Is Truthful:

When you teach your children, it is important to teach them the truth because the truth can set them free from ignorance, failure, darkness, pain, shame, and the regrets of life. This means, you want to make sure you are teaching them the truth about every subject matter. *John 8:32 (NIV) teaches us thus, "and you will know the truth, and the truth will set you free."*

Teaching children the truth about life empowers them for a strong future so they can navigate and secure their life in God. As a parent who loves and wants the best for their child, it is important to partner with the Spirit of truth to lead you into all truths as you teach them.

A Teacher Is Empathetic:

The ability to be empathetic helps you and your children connect during their learning process. Dr. Brene Brown says this about empathy, and I quote, "Empathy is climbing down to where they are and saying, 'I know what it's like down here.'[6] It's important to reach inwards to remember your childhood experiences to help you walk in their shoes. We were once children, we remember how the adults made us feel; it's therefore important to be empathetic when teaching our children.

Empathy is an essential skill to have as a parent because it enables us to connect emotionally with our children. It gives children the reassurances that they are not alone but belong to a loving family. God made you go through all the stages of childhood before sending you a child to take care of. He wanted you to feel what they would one day feel so you could be empathetic to your children.

Empathy forces you to lower unrealistic expectations, while increasing your compassion quotient so you can focus more on helping people navigate through the challenges they face on every stage of growth.

Being empathetic when teaching your children involves the following:

- Giving them your 100 percent attention when listening to them.
- Engaging with your body language; that is, eye contact, nodding your head and smiling to show you respect and acknowledge them.

- Ensuring they know that you believe in them and are committed to help them believe in themselves..

Theodore Roosevelt said this: "Nobody cares how much you know, until they know how much you care."

A Teacher Is Authentic:

Being authentic is a great way to build connections while teaching your children. Don't be uppity, stoic and perfect; always remember you were once a child; you messed up some time, you failed, and you were corrected by your loving parents or other adults. Relax. Let your children know you as a person. Being authentic lets your children know you. It reminds them that you once passed their present stage and grew into who you presently are. That, there is hope!

Feel free to share your stories with your children in age-appropriate bites. You want them to know you authentically not scare or scar them. Tell them about your days in school, who your favorite teacher in school was, your favorite subject, your most embarrassing experience, and the fear and struggles you ever had as a child. Laugh hard about them and be real because, it is a great way to build lasting memories that will empower them with inner strength as they grow.

This is a quote by Roy T. Bennett: "If you don't know who you truly are, you'll never know what you really want."

A Teacher Is Caring:

Caring is to ensure that someone is well, safe, and well nurtured. Caring here involves ensuring that a child is empowered and equipped for the future with the knowledge they need to succeed and advance in life. Caring for people makes them feel loved and accepted, and the act of caring for others comes with a lot of rewards. Caring for a child builds a strong connection between you and the child, it makes you feel fulfilled, improves your self-esteem, and gives you a sense of accomplishment.

"They may forget what you said, but they will never forget how you made them feel."

—*Carl W. Buechner*[9]

A Teacher is Helpful:

Teachers are helpers. They train, show the way, and empower people to grow from one stage to the other—we always need helpers. Helping a child through teaching can make a huge difference in their lives forever.

Here are some benefits of helping children:

- Helping children boosts your mood and ultimately makes you to be more optimistic and positive of your children.
- Helping children can help you live a fulfilled life knowing you empowered a little one.

- You get to also build a lasting bond between you and them.
- Helping your children makes you improve on yourself as you want to be worthy of the honor.

"Somewhere along the way, we must learn that there is nothing greater than to do something for others."
—*Martin Luther King Jr.*[8]

A Teacher Is Encouraging:

Children crave for words of encouragement, praise, and support from the adults they respect. This in turn can motivate and drive them to be successful in life. Let's take a closer look at the word **encourage;** you will find the word **courage** within **it**. To encourage children means to empower them with courage. We see in the Bible that God Himself empowered the children of Israel with courage.

"Be strong and courageous" He said. (Deut. 31:6 NIV).

Hebrews 3:13 (NIV) tells us: *"But encourage one another daily, as long as it is called "Today," so that none of you may be hardened by sin's deceitfulness."* Paul the apostle is instructing us to encourage each other every day because it can empower us to overcome life's challenges. It is important to know that every day, children need courage to stand up for what is right, make wise choices, and overcome the struggles of their age, everywhere. We must be determined as parents to encourage them to be the best in all they do.

I love to encourage parents to consciously speak encouragement in the atmosphere of their home. Let it be like oxygen in the air for your children so they can breathe it in daily. Remind them of who they are and what they can do, nudge them gently when you find them doing wrong. Correction must be done with a balance called encouragement.

Here are some benefits of encouraging and empowering our children with courage:

- Encouraging your children empowers them to excel in their endeavors.
- It strengthens them to face the challenges of life, take on difficult tasks, and do their assignments with tenacity.
- It keeps children positive and makes them optimistic about life.
- It strengthens the bond between you and your children.
- It empowers your children to honor you.
- It empowers them to preserve in life.

A Teacher Is Role Model:

As children grow, parents play an essential part in their positive development. They influence their values, behavior, and attitude. As positive role models, we must constantly and deliberately stay present in the lives of our children, inspiring and living a meaningful life.

Teaching positions you strategically to be your child's role model.

Children are great at mimicking others. They learn by example from the people around them. We must deliberately position ourselves as positive role models early in their lives, living with integrity, optimism, hope, determination, and compassion. We must strive to treat others with kindness, fairness, consideration, and truthfulness. This allows them to not only learn but also love and respect us as they grow.

As children grow, they will have other role models in their lives besides us who will influence them, it is therefore important to position ourselves as positive role models because they may not know all of their role models personally for experiential impact. Let your love for them and presence in their lives position you as a positive and worthy role model to help balance out wrong influences.

Here are some benefits of why you should be a role model:

- You get to bring balance in your child's life.
- You have tremendous impact in their lives.

- You feel fulfilled as you motivate and inspire your children in life.
- You become better as you live your life conscious that you are influencing someone.

Teaching positions you to be respected by your children. Role modeling is a powerful way of teaching your children the knowledge, skills, and values of life.

"We must acknowledge…that the most important, indeed the only, thing we have to offer our students is ourselves. Everything else they can read in a book."

—*D. C. Tosteson*[7]

The importance of teaching children cannot be overemphasized. Many great adults today are who they are because of a teacher who spoke the right words to them; a teacher who showed them how to do some things; a teacher who believed in them when other people did not see their potential; a teacher who was deliberate to connect, impact, build, and lead the way; and a teacher who empowered them with knowledge to become.

Children are born blank and clueless about life; it's our place as parents to acknowledge this and teach them how to live life here on earth. When we teach our children important skills and values of life, we are taking them from darkness, which is ignorance, to empowering and equipping them with knowledge, which is light and power. They grow to become caring, responsible, and well-rounded adults.

Feel free to use the lists in this book as references or checklists to investigate what needs to be taught or strengthened in your child's journey.

CHAPTER 4
Every Child Desires a Teacher

"Everyone has the right to be taught, including your child."
—Nene Oluwagbohun

"Never miss an opportunity to teach, when you teach others, you teach yourself."
—Itzhak Perlman [10]

"Teach these things and insist that everyone learn them."
—1 Timothy 4:11 (NLT)

Every child desire to have a

T—Truthful,
E—Empathetic,
A—Authentic,
C—Caring,
H—Helpful,
E—Encouraging, and
R—Role Model— *teacher* in their lives.

Recent research commissioned by YMCA and conducted by a poll of about 2,000 parents, showed what many parents wish they could teach their children. Most wished they could teach them life skills. Results recently shows that 75 percent of life skill lessons are commonly taught by parents and the YMCA research revealed that most parents are worried that they have not been able to teach their children these life skill lessons because of life's demands.[11]

This research also reveals the dissatisfaction parents feel when they are not involved in teaching their children life-skills that has the potentials to empower them for the future. For instance, in the research I mentioned above, some wished they could teach their children digital safety- something that has become a necessity in our society today. There is a deep-rooted satisfaction that comes with teaching and empowering our children ourselves because that is how it has been designed by nature and it is a command from the creator. Deuteronomy 6:7 (ESV) says: *"You shall teach them diligently to your children and shall talk of them when you sit in your house, and when you walk by the way, and when you lie down, and when you rise."*

This does not just mean teaching them the Word of God only; it also means teaching them life skills(the Word of God contains lessons for life skills everyone needs). Teaching is one of the patterns designed by God for training a child. Therefore, any parent, who wants to follow the pattern of God, must teach their children. The teaching pattern is designed to impact, train, empower, build, encourage, and prepare our children for their life's purpose and assignment.

In the royal families, there is a pattern for raising royalty from birth. Royal babies are born with a sense of purpose because they represent a kingdom. Every child born into a palace as royalty is taught kingdom etiquettes from toddlerhood. Topics range from dress codes, to their gait, and everything in between because they represent the kingdom.

We belong to the kingdom of God where God is King. He created and made us His most prized creatures. He also has a pattern He has prepared for us because we represent Him here on earth.

Patterns are authorized formularies used to get the desired results. God has designed teaching as a formulary used in raising children to be great and outstanding. The pattern of God is far above any cultural, tribal, and national pattern. As we follow His pattern for training our children, we will enjoy peace, favor, and outstanding results in the lives of our children and have rest in our lives also. It is apparent that we must deliberately make time to teach our children Godly principles, rules, and the mechanics for living life here on earth.

Deep inside every child is a desire to be taught; they desire to have someone teach them, and they cannot know without being taught. Romans 10:14 (NIV) asks, "...*and how can they hear about him unless someone tells them?"* There is a need for them to be taught, and they have a right to be taught by their parents.

The devil's desire is to keep us so busy we do not find time to train our children. It is often easier to let them operate in ignorance. We play into his sinister plot when we leave our children to ignorance because this exposes them to many who do not have their best interests at heart. They lead them astray to make foolish and unwise decisions that come with great consequences.

Hosea 4:6 (NIV) laments: *"My people are destroyed for lack of knowledge."*

When Jesus gathered His disciples, he started teaching them. See in Mark 8:31(NIV): *"He then began to teach them."* We must be present in our children's lives so we can teach them. Our children are royalty; they are God's precious and valuable possession. Psalm 127:3 reiterates this, it says; "Children are a heritage from the LORD, offspring a reward from him." We are responsible for what we make out of this valuable possession. We must reintroduce them to their Father, the one who owns them and helps them live a victorious life here on earth.

Just like bad teaching can destroy, good teaching can give life. In my career as a life coach to many young children, I have come to realize that there is a deep cry in every child yearning for a teacher, an instructor, a good leader, and a coach who is willing to teach them the right thing. There are ongoing concerns and worries among parents and caregivers about the high rate of children's exposure to porn, drugs, gangs, prostitution, and the many evils around. This is because many parents and guardians are absent from their children's lives, especially during the learning stages of their lives. Those who are present must engage in teaching and encouraging the children, not assuming they know or should know, or that maybe someone else would teach them.

We are to be careful not to assume or expect that our children will know things we didn't teach them. This could lead to frustration and anger in the relationship. It could also cause depression in teenagers as well as fester the feeling of inadequacy. It is therefore very important to be patient as you teach them.

Try not to put yourself or your children under unnecessary pressure by asking them to behave in a way you never taught them.. You may end up feeling disappointed, angry, worried, and embarrassed.

Teaching enhances the relationship between you and your child, and empowers your children to give back when the need arises for the action. Teaching does not always need to be done sitting and lecturing; the book of Deuteronomy 11:19 tells us how to teach them.

How to Teach Your Children

"Teach them to your children, talking about them when you sit at home and when you walk along the road, when you lie down and when you get up" (Deut. 11:19 NIV).

It says:

- Teach when you sit, (in the living room, during morning devotional, while watching a television program, when sitting in the car, in church, sitting in dining room for lunch or dinner, in class, and so forth).

- Teach when you walk (on the road, driving to a destination, and so forth). I do this a lot when my husband and I are driving our children to school; we listen to short motivational talks from YouTube connected to the car's Bluetooth, and we discuss it. The motivational talk could be on one of our family's values, like honesty, time management, focus, prayers, and so forth. Sometimes we listen to a chapter of an audio book and have a short conversation on it. When on a road trip, we listen to books too.

- Teach it when you lie down. Having a Bluetooth in your children's room that reads the scripture to them as they lie down to sleep is a great way to have them rest their mind on the Word of God. Some recent scientific research has shown that people who listen to music or audio books significantly increase their rested state during sleep, improving their cognitive performance, fight diseases, and shorten the time their brain waves shut down. How much more when our children sleep with the Word of God playing all through the night, creating an atmosphere that allows their spirits interact with the Father of all spirits.

- Teach it when you get up. The brain functions with the first information it encounters within the first fifteen minutes of waking up. If it is good information, that determines a lot about how motivated a person will be; and if it is negative information, it will demotivate the person throughout the day. Teach your children the Word of God first thing every morning. The moment my children started reading fluently, I started buying them age-appropriate devotionals so they could study the scriptures by themselves every morning. So, when they wake up, they study the devotional first. This is a practice that they will carry into their adulthood, so it is therefore important to start practicing it now when they are young, as we equip them with resources that will enable them to study the Word of God independently. It gives them a great time to interact with God alone first before the start of their day, and we will worry less about their spirituality as they leave home.

When we start early to teach them the importance of the Word of God and give them an independent environment to do it themselves as we do with other things like their schoolwork, we will create an environment for the Holy Spirit to work in them, while they begin their walk early and grow a personal relationship with Him. This does not rule out coming together to have family devotion from time to time—please do. This idea of having our children study the Word of God on their own helps rule out the excuse of no time to study and helps our children prioritize their day and time effectively.

When the children have all the resources they need to study the Word and time allocated to that each day, they will do it joyfully, and you will worry less about their spiritual growth. I also encourage parents to check how they are doing, from time to time as you drive to school or have breakfast. For instance, ask about what they read and what they understood from it. That is a great way to build family teaching topics.

Teaching will require investing a lot of time, but at the end, you will be forever grateful and pleased you did it, as you see them independent, happy, mature, empowered, and brave to face life's challenges and be victorious. Every child has a right to be taught, and there are lots of things you can begin teaching your children from an early age.

CHAPTER 5

Teach Spiritual Matter

"Each day of our lives we make deposits in the memory banks of our children."

—Chuck Swindoll[12]

"Every one of our children will be brought into the ark if we pray and work earnestly for them."

—Dwight L. Moody[13]

*"Train up a child in **the way** he should go, And when he is old he will not depart from it."*

—Proverbs 22:6 9 (KJV)

"Every child is a spirit, they are ageless and ancient, and they desire to be taught about their ageless Father while on earth."

—Nene Oluwagbohun

Proverbs 22:6 9 (KJV) reveals to us that training is time bond for a child. There is a set time for training up a child. But most parents miss out on the time of training. The time of training is a crucial season of a child's life, a particular season of raising a child. When we fail to engage our children in the season when they are teachable and malleable, it becomes difficult to do it when they are fully formed by other opinions and mindsets, this will definitely lead to a clash harming our relationship with the child.

Training is a deliberate art that must be done consciously and carefully, bearing in mind that it is time sensitive. As a parent, you have the first responsibility to teach your child because they are plain fields that need cultivation. Note that whether you cultivate their field or not, something will definitely grow. We must be deliberate about the seeds that need to be planted in the field of our children's hearts. If we plant good seeds and nurture them, they will grow into trees that bear good fruits for a better world where lost and hungry individuals can find good fruits to eat from.

Plant the Seed of the Knowledge of God

Hebrew 12:9 asks, *"How much more should we submit to the Father of spirits and live?"*

Everyone is a spirit, and God is the Father of all spirits. It is important to teach your children early in life about their spiritual and eternal Father- the one from whom they originated from through training them up in ***the way*** and according to

John 14:6 (NIV) *"Jesus answered, "I am **the way** and the truth and the life. No one comes to the Father except through me.*

*Proverbs 22:6 9 (KJV) instructs us to "Train up a child in **the way** he should go, and when he is old he will not depart from it."* This scriptures tells that when our children are trained up in **the way**, (Jesus) we are rest assured of their future.

Every child existed as a spirit before they came to earth. Jeremiah 1:5 tells us, *"Before I formed you in the womb I knew you, before you were born, I set you apart; I appointed you as a prophet to the nations."*

A prophet is one who tells others the mind of God. Everyone created is created to express the mind of God in one way or the other on earth. This means that children are packaged as **purposes** deployed to the earth because everything God creates is designed to serve a purpose for Him. Proverbs 16:4 (NIV) says, *"The LORD has made everything for its purpose."*

It is very interesting how as parents, we do not even have a full picture of our own purpose; let alone our children's purpose and assignment. The beautiful thing is, as we partner with God in a deliberate relationship, He will begin to reveal this purpose to us in small bites. He then also reveals that of our children's to enable us raise our children accordingly. We see an example of this in the Bible with Manoah and his wife. This couple had been married and could not bear children. They asked God for a child, and one day an angel of the Lord came to them to tell them about the child Samson. They did not just say; "Okay, thank you." They probed for clarity and also asked for help.

Yes Indeed! They asked for help, as can be seen in Judges13:8 (NIV): *"Then Manoah prayed to the Lord: 'Pardon your servant, Lord. I beg you to let the man of God you sent to us come **again to teach us how to bring up the boy who is to be born.**'"*

God will always hear our cry for help. God heard this man's cry for help and sent the angel back to him with answers.

God heard Manoah, and the angel of God came again to the woman *while she was out in the field; but her husband Manoah was not with her.* [10] *The woman hurried to tell her husband, "He's here! The man who appeared to me the other day!"* [11] *Manoah got up and followed his wife. When he came to the man, he said, "Are you the man who talked to my wife?"* (Judg. 13:9–11 NIV)

He unashamedly asked for *how* to raise the child. As kingdom parents, we must ask God to teach us how to nurture, each child sent to us. This is where partnering with God, the giver of every child, is so important. Judges 13:12 (NIV) says, *"'I am,' he said.12 So Manoah asked him, '**When your words are fulfilled, what is to be the rule that governs the boy's life and work?**'"*

This is so important because every child is deployed to the earth with a unique purpose and assignment. The ability to help lead them right can only come by partnering with God, the boss Himself so each child can be raised to fulfill their God-given assignment and purpose.

We cannot parent our children in the way God desires us to without a living relationship with Him. A living relationship reveals His heart and intentions to us every day as we deliberately walk with Him; just as we read in Judges 13 about Samson.

Before Samson was born, there was a 40 year long war between Israel and the Philistine because of their evil deeds. I am sure some Israelites called out to God for mercy to deliver them. And God heard them and deployed Samson for this assignment. His parents knew this child was not ordinary, and so they asked how he should be raised to fit into this assignment he had come to carry out—and they were told how—see that in verse 12.

Someone once said to me, "Every child has a purpose and is born for the season with a specific assignment for their time." Could it be that your child is born for a specific assignment for such a time as this? I strongly believe Manoah and his wife taught Samson who he was and who God was to Him. They must have made him understand how much he needed to depend on God. I am sure the truth of Philippians 4:13, *"I can do all things through Christ who strengthens me,"* became a reality to Samson as he grew.

Judges 13:24–25 continues: *"He grew and the Lord blessed him, 25 and the Spirit of the Lord began to stir him while he was in Mahaneh Dan, between Zorah and Eshtaol".*

The word *grew* in Hebrew means to expand, but it has lot of other explanations. I would like to go with this explanation: "to cultivate by growing, often involving improvements by means of agricultural techniques." This means in the process of Samson's growth, his parents were cultivating his heart with the knowledge of God, and there came the blessings of God upon him. When we teach our children about God, it comes with a blessing. We will always see the evidence in their lives. I imagine that their teaching also gave the Holy Spirit His place to stir him up. Everything He did in all those cities was stirred up by the Spirit of God.

There are some secrets you must know as you raise your children with the knowledge of God.

Always know that God is in control—see Judges 14:1–4:

> *Samson went down to Timnah and saw there a young Philistine woman. 2 When he returned, he said to his father and mother, "I have seen a Philistine woman in Timnah; now get her for me as my wife." 3 His father and mother replied, "Isn't there*

an acceptable woman among your relatives or among all our people? Must you go to the uncircumcised Philistines to get a wife?" But Samson said to his father, "Get her for me. She's the right one for me." 4 (His parents did not know that this was from the Lord, who was seeking an occasion to confront the Philistines; for at that time, they were ruling over Israel.)

His parents wanted to use traditions of the past, but God had a plan, and they did not see it. We must learn to depend on God totally. The moment our children begin to experience God for themselves, we must learn to totally trust God for them too. Some things may seem overwhelming, but just trust God and keep praying for them. Many parents begin to see everything from the negative, out of fear. No, just pause; it may just be the path ordained by God that they need to go through. We see that in Samson's life. It was God's plan and strategy to get the Philistines into the hands of the Israelites.

After teaching our children, we must learn to step back and keep praying for them, especially when they are done with their season of teaching. Now in the coaching season of their lives, you must be ready to trust and believe in God. We will talk more about the coaching season of our children's lives in future chapters.

Jesus Christ went through that part; it was what was written in the volumes of His books about Him. He needed to fulfill every word. Samson was born for that period in Israel's history.

Our place is to walk with the Father, introduce our children to the Father, receive wisdom to teach them, and then step back and let God lead.

Your biggest responsibility is to reintroduce them to their heavenly father, who entrusted you with them to take care of. You reintroduce them back to God as they arrive on the earth through Jesus Christ. We must teach them about the love of God displayed through Jesus to mankind, designed to reunite us to Him so that we can be saved and reunited. That is ***the only way*** they can begin to discover themselves and live their purpose. As soon as they begin to talk and communicate, dive into reintroducing them back to God. Create a pathway in their brain for the knowledge of God on time, before they begin to learn other things.

Be selective about the kinds of music, movies, games, activities and resources you expose them to so as not to corrupt them unknowingly. Choose wisely and start on time too to help them guide their minds in things that will help them become impactful on earth.

> "Above all else, guard your heart, for everything you do flows from it."
> —*Proverbs 4:23 NIV*

Teaching our children about God on time is a process of cultivating their mind so they can grow spiritually, emotionally, mentally, and physically sound. We see this in Samson, In Jesus Christ and Samuel, Daniel, David, Esther, Deborah, and many others in the scriptures, their hearts were cultivated and the seed of God was planted first in them, and you will read what followed after—and the Lord was with them.

> 1 Samuel 3:19 (NIV) *"**The LORD was with Samuel** as he grew up, and he let none of Samuel's words fall to the ground"*
>
> Luke 2:40 (NIV) *"And the child grew and became strong; he was filled with wisdom, **and the grace of God was on him.**"*

I believe Daniel and his friends were taught about God on time; that they were reintroduced to the Father of all spirits and were taught about Him while they were still young. They were grounded in the Word so that when they found themselves in Babylon as young men (teenagers), they remembered what was taught them. They believed it and stood by it and God showed up.

> *Then Daniel talked to the guard who had been put in charge of Daniel, Hananiah, Mishael, and Azariah by Ashpenaz. He said, "Please give us this test for ten days: Don't give us anything but vegetables to eat and water to drink. Then after ten days, compare us with the other young men who eat the king's food. See for yourself who looks healthier, and then decide how you want to treat us, your servants." So the guard agreed to test Daniel, Hananiah, Mishael, and Azariah for ten days. After*

> *ten days, Daniel and his friends looked healthier than all the young men who ate the king's food. So the guard continued to take away the king's special food and wine and to give only vegetables to Daniel, Hananiah, Mishael, and Azariah.* **God gave these four young men the wisdom and ability to learn many kinds of writing and science. Daniel could also understand all kinds of visions and dreams.** (Dan. 1:11–17 ERV)

In those days, the animals served as food at the king's palaces were animal sacrificed to an idol. The leftovers were prepared as meals for the boys. They were not fooled or tempted into eating food dedicated to idols, they rejected the meals because of God's command against eating such meals.

They also understood the importance of fasting and feasting on vegetables, they knew that these would renew and rejuvenate them. This was as a result of them being taught.

Many of us fail to teach our children because we limit them in our minds. We think they are too young to understand the deep things of God. It would amaze you to find how the things you have taught them will come alive when life calls, be sure it will save them from lots of troubles when you aren't there.

> "My people are destroyed for lack of knowledge."
> —Hosea 4:6 (KJV)

Trust in God and don't be ignorant; teach them about their Father God and His Word and watch Him do what He wants to do with your children. Never forget that He created them and sent them to earth for His own purpose.

Plant the Seed of Their Identity: Yes, teach them about their identities. We are in a generation where uncertainty and confusion is the order of the day. People have lost their sense of identity; it is pertinent that we must teach our children about their identities. Their identities must be rooted in God their Creator and the Father of all spirits, where they originated from. First, our children are made in the image and likeness of God and must be taught to know that they are like God in every form.

When you say someone is made in an *image*, it means the person is a duplicate of the original. When we say they are made in the *likeness*, it means they are made just to reflect the same thing.

We are made to be like God here on earth. We look like Him in the spirit because we are first spirits.

We are made male or female to represent God here on earth. There are things we were never given the opportunity to choose before we arrived earth; we have no control over who our parents are, the families we belong to, our nationality, our skin color, our tribe, and more. We were not even given the choice to choose our gender. God chose to send us here on earth to represent Him just the way He made us (male or female). Mark 10:6 says, *"But at the beginning of creation God 'made them male and female.'"*

Our children must be comfortable and pleased to represent God just as they are. This scripture here defines the sovereignty of God over man. We can't question Him or challenge Him about His choices for us. We must teach our children to be comfortable and be at peace with their gender.

For many who are questioning this, even neuroscientists have found out that men and women have different brain formations and make up, and that each serves different purposes, processing things differently. We may want to change the physical look, but what happens to the brain?

When humans fail to function in the full capacity of their makeup, they become confused and depressed. These are real consequences of life. We must help our children avoid these.

> *They exchanged the truth about God for a lie, and worshiped and served created things rather than the Creator—who is forever praised. Amen. Because of this, God gave them over to shameful lusts. Even their women exchanged natural sexual relations for unnatural ones. In the same way the men also abandoned natural relations with women and were inflamed with lust for one another. Men committed shameful acts with*

> *other men, and received in themselves the due penalty for their error. Furthermore, just as they did not think it worthwhile to retain the knowledge of God, so God gave them over to a depraved mind, so that they do what ought not to be done. They have become filled with every kind of wickedness, evil, greed and depravity. They are full of envy, murder, strife, deceit and malice. They are gossips, slanderers, God-haters, insolent, arrogant and boastful; they invent ways of doing evil; they disobey their parents; they have no understanding, no fidelity, no love, no mercy.* (Rom. 1:25–30 NIV)

As parents, God has chosen and sent us to nurture and groom the children He gave to us. We must be conscious to continually reaffirm who God is to our children and who He has called them to be- that is what defines their identity on earth.

They must not forget that they are the following:

> *But you are a chosen people, a royal priesthood, a holy nation, God's special possession, that you may declare the praises of him who called you out of darkness into his wonderful light.*
> —1 Peter 2:9

- Chosen people of God (deployed for a purpose).
- They are royalty because their Father is King.
- They are priests who reconcile others to God by their words and actions.
- They are holy.

- They are special treasures to God.
- They are the sons and daughters of God. 2 Corinthians 6:18 (NIV) states: *"I will be a Father to you, and you will be my sons and daughters, says the Lord Almighty."*
- They are His offspring. Acts 17:28 (NIV) assures us: *"For in him we live and move and have our being. 'As some of your own poets have said, 'We are his offspring.'"*
- They are part of the family of God through the blood as they believe in Him. Ephesians 3:14–15, 14 (NIV) says, *"For this reason I kneel before the Father, 15 from whom every family in heaven and on earth derives its name,"* and John 1:12 (NIV) says, *"Yet to all who did receive him, to those who believed in his name, he gave the right to become children of God."*
- They are ambassadors of God's Kingdom here on earth. 2 Corinthians 5:20 says, *"We are therefore Christ's ambassadors, as though God were making his appeal through us. We implore you on Christ's behalf: Be reconciled to God."*
- They are loved with an everlasting love by the heavenly Father who is love personified. In Jeremiah 31:3 (NIV) He declares His love for us when He said: *"…I have loved you with an everlasting love; I have drawn you with unfailing kindness."* First John 4:8 (NIV) tells us: *"…because God is love."*
- They have the Holy Spirit in them who teaches them all things, showing them all things and things to come.

> *But very truly I tell you, it is for your good that I am going away. Unless I go away, the Advocate will not come to you; but if I go, I will send him to you. 8 When he comes, he will prove the world to be in the wrong about sin and righteousness and judgment: 9 about sin, because people do not believe in me; 10 about righteousness, because I am going to the Father, where you can see me no longer; 11 and about judgment, because the prince of this world now stands condemned. 12 "I have much more to say to you, more than you can now bear.* **13 But when he, the Spirit of truth, comes, he will guide you into all the truth. He will not speak on his own; he will speak only what he hears, and he will tell you what is yet to come. 14 He will glorify me because it is from me that he will receive what he will make known to you.** *15 All that belongs to the Father is mine. That is why I said the Spirit will receive from me what he will make known to you.* (John 16:7–15, 7)

In John 14:15–26, Jesus tells us:

> *If you love me, keep my commands. 16 And I will ask the Father, and he will give you another advocate to help you and be with you forever—17 the Spirit of truth. The world cannot accept him, because it neither sees him nor knows him. But you know him, for he lives with you and will be[a] in you. 18 I will not leave you as orphans; I will come to you. 19 Before long, the world will not see me anymore, but you will see me. Because I live, you also will live. 20 On that day you will realize that I am in my Father, and you are in me, and I am in you. 21 Whoever*

has my commands and keeps them is the one who loves me. The one who loves me will be loved by my Father, and I too will love them and show myself to them." 22 Then Judas (not Judas Iscariot) said, "But, Lord, why do you intend to show yourself to us and not to the world?" 23 Jesus replied, "Anyone who loves me will obey my teaching. My Father will love them, and we will come to them and make our home with them. 24 Anyone who does not love me will not obey my teaching. These words you hear are not my own; they belong to the Father who sent me. 25 "All this I have spoken while still with you. 26 But the Advocate, the Holy Spirit, whom the Father will send in my name, will teach you all things and will remind you of everything I have said to you.

Our children must understand their identity, and they must be taught that this is how God sees them. They are not royalty because they were born into a physical royal home, but because their heavenly Father to whom they will return to someday is *King*. As expected, the only thing required of them is to let Him love on them, as they accept His love while obeying his instructions and commandments.

John 14:15 says, *"If you love me, keep my commands."*

Teach your children that they are created for a purpose: The Word of God says that everything God created is for a purpose. Yes, they are created for a purpose by the Manufacturer who is God. They are for His purpose, as Proverbs 16:4 (NIV) says:

"The LORD has made everything for its purpose." He conceived us in His plans and deployed us uniquely to represent Him and serve a special purpose here on earth.

Purpose here simply means; *reason*. We must teach our children to know that they were made for a special reason. They must see themselves as precious products, uniquely and terrifically designed to carry out a special assignment for God. Let them know that they cannot discover or live out this purpose without a relationship with the God who made them. He has that purpose written in the volume of the books written concerning each of us, and we cannot have access to this essence of this book unless we have a relationship with Him.

Psalm 40:7 says, *"Then said I, Lo, I come: in the volume of the book it is written of me."*

Hebrews 10:7 says, *"Then I said, 'Here I am—it is written about me in the scroll—I have come to do your will, my God.'"*

These scriptures also speak of the book written about each of us. There is a book written about you and about your children. Predestined in Him are these books written, and it is our choice to open them by having a relationship with Him. For your children to fulfill this purpose, according to what is written in the books, they need to have a personal relationship with God. Nobody can investigate or access the book or live their lives for them. They must submit their will willingly to

Him, make the choice to follow Him, and walk with the Holy Spirit to enjoy the bond of a personal relationship with God.

According to Ephesians 1:5, *"He predestined us for adoption to sonship through Jesus Christ, in accordance with His pleasure and will."*

One day as I was teaching my children about the Lord, He showed me two books and said to me, "There are two books written for each person before they were born. Just like (the tree of life and the tree of death in Genesis), there is the book of life and the book of death. Our choices determine which book we will live out here on earth. Each book has its contents. There is a book containing the blessing; if we choose to follow Him and obey His commands and there is the other book that contains the consequences of disobeying His commands. The book of life contains lots of beautiful promises and blessings of peace, joy, love, wealth, grace, prosperity, wisdom, light, increase rest, power, and favor, etc; and the book of death contains curses that will result in pain, shame, confusion, depression, diseases, poverty, loneliness, and death at the end. Every human is given a gift called the power of *choice* or *will* when they arrive on earth. How we use our choices determines what kind of life we will live here on earth—a life of blessings or a life of sorrow and pain.

> *"This day I call the heavens and the earth as witnesses against you that I have set before you life and death, blessings, and*

curses. Now choose life, so that you and your children may live"
(Deut. 30:19 NIV).

*"But you must not eat from the tree of the knowledge of good and evil, for **when** you eat from it you will certainly die"* (Gen. 2:17 NIV).

The word **when** speaks of choice.

Another version English Revised Version (ERV) says in Genesis 2:17" *but of the tree of the knowledge of good and evil, thou shalt not eat of it: **for in the day that thou eatest** thereof thou shalt surely die."*

"For the day that thou eatest" means the day you chose to eat that tree, you will die. We see that from the beginning, God gave man the power to make their choices. What Adam and Eve experienced was based on the choices they made.

When we choose to submit our will to obey Him, the book of life is opened unto us. This ripples into enjoying loads of benefits just because of the choice we made- A blessed life of ultimate joy that comes to us despite the troubles going on around us, we enjoy ultimate Joy, Peace, enjoyment and fulfillment. However, if we forsake Him and submit our will to obeying the evil one, we will suffer the pain, shame, depression, sadness, and rejection of life written in the book of death.

Revelation 20:12 says, *"And I saw the dead, great and small, standing before the throne, and **books** were opened. Another book was opened, which is the book of life. The dead were judged according to what they had done as recorded in the books."*

As parents, we must continually walk with our heavenly Father, while teaching our children to submit their will to make the right choices so we can enjoy the blessings that flow from our beautiful relationship with the Father.

Many will say, "I do not know how to teach my child the Word or spiritual matters," but I say, don't be troubled. Once you are saved, I tell you, you have the mind of Christ and the Holy Spirit is with you, to teach you all things. He is willing to help you. Ask Him. He may lead you to a Bible story. As you pick up the story from the Bible to read to them, allow the Holy Spirit make it come alive to do His work

And if you are not saved and you are a parent reading this book, please don't panic or wonder about where to begin; you can start even right now as I encourage you to believe that God loves you and has great thoughts and plans for you. He has said in Jeremiah 29;11 (NIV), *"For I know the plans I have for you,"* declares the Lord, *"plans to prosper you and not to harm you, plans to give you hope and a future."* And in Psalm 139:17-18 (NKJV) **"How precious also are Your thoughts to me, O God! How great is the sum of them! 18 If I should count them, they** *would be more in number than the sand; When I awake, I am still with You."*

All you need to do is believe that He died and rose again and declare it with your mouth. You will be saved, and it will be a great and new start for you, as Romans 10:9 says: *"If you declare with your mouth, "Jesus is Lord," and believe in your heart that God raised him from the dead, you will be saved."*

Did you do this? Yes!

Congratulations and welcome home! We join the host of heaven in celebration of your choice; we rejoice because there is rejoicing in heaven right now over you. Luke 15:7 (NKJV) says, *"I tell you that in the same way there will be more rejoicing in heaven over one sinner who repents than over ninety-nine righteous persons who do not need to repent."*

Wow, there is joy in heaven over you. Your heavenly Father is throwing a party over your return to Him! The angels and the host of heaven are rejoicing over you—and I am also joining them to rejoice over you.

Wow, welcome home, and God bless you. It's going to be a beautiful ride as you stay with Him. You are now on the winning team.

I will also love to encourage you to find a faith-based community of children of God and connect, and you can email us here; (neneolu@gmail.com) so we can keep you in our prayers. God bless you. Welcome again to the *kingdom* and the community of kingdom parents who are deliberately raising *kingdom-minded children*.

CHAPTER 6

Teach Values of Life

"Your beliefs become your thoughts, your thoughts become your words, Your words become your actions, Your actions become your habits, Your habits become your values, Your values become your destiny."

—Gandhi[14]

"What you teach your children becomes their beliefs, their beliefs become their thoughts, and their thoughts wrapped in their imaginations become what they live out as their values, to make the world a better or worse place."

—Nene Oluwagbohun

"For when Gentiles, who do not have the law, by nature do what the law requires, they are a law to themselves, even though they do not have the law. They show that the work of the law is written on their hearts, while their conscience also bears witness, and their conflicting thoughts accuse or even excuse them."

—Romans 2:14–15

> "For the past thirty-three years, I have looked in the mirror every morning and asked myself, 'If today were the last day of my life, would I want to do what I am about to do today?' And whenever the answer has been 'No' for too many days in a row, I know I need to change something."
>
> —Steve Jobs[15]

Morals are standards of behavior or a belief about what is acceptable in the society. Morals are general standards of living. For instance, you love to be respected; you also love to work with honest people, right? It's the same with everyone else, no matter where they are.

We must be deliberate about teaching our children morals from home. This could be done through short stories because we learn a lot from story books, fairy tales, and stories from the Bible. Here are some important morals you can teach your children:

- Honesty: is the importance of telling the truth. Being truthful pays off and strengthens relationships with others. The list does not stop here, for we are also taught that—
- Integrity has great reward.
- It is important to treat others with respect.
- Hard work pays greatly.
- Endurance and patience is rewarding
- Failing is also a learning process to achieving success.

- Loving and obeying God is greatly rewarding.
- Loving others is important in life; it makes the world a better place.
- Teach your children that life is governed by principles. What you give is what comes back to us. Also teach them:
- The importance of forgiveness and how forgiveness improves our health.
- Time management. How time is a currency you invest, and what you invest into determines how your life turns out.
- We must teach our children to stay focused and always be grateful because that keeps them mentally strong.
- Collaboration and teamwork are important.
- Sharing is important.

Empathy

Empathy is the ability for one to use their imagination to compassionately feel how others feel or see their experience or situation. It is the ability to feel the emotions of others; it is the ability to consider others. For instance, children have very high ability to feel the emotions of others; that is why, children can cry when they see others crying. That is why they say "sorry" to the person crying. When raising a self-confident child, it is important to raise a child with empathy because children with empathy will grow to become more self-aware and bold, this will in turn help them connect with others as they develop great social skills to become great leaders.

Here are some ways to teach children empathy:

Ask them how they feel from time to time and encourage them to **name** their feelings. If they feel happy, let them name it; if they feel sad, let them name it. This will help them connect with what they feel and understand what it means.

- Being available and genuinely connecting with them during conversations.
- Give them undivided attention during conversations.
- Remember to make eye contact and use other body languages to connect during conversations.
- Teach them how to connect with other people by engaging in interactions like responding to questions when asked.
- Show and teach them about Gods empathetic nature. Let them know that God sent His only begotten Son to die on the cross for us so we can connect to Him (John 3:16 KJV).
- Show them how God sent Jesus to die in exchange for our sins because He knew we would never be able to provide a befitting sacrifice for our sins.
- Letting them always know that the Holy Spirit is there to help them.

Empathy is a strong skill every child needs to learn to function well and productively in life. Empathy gives people an opportunity to experience love, care, trust, and hope.

Teach Your Children Financial Intelligence: Financial intelligence is the ability to acquire financial education. Knowledge on assets and liabilities is fundamental to attaining financial freedom, but it starts with wealth. Wealth is having all you need to be successful. *"His divine power has given us everything we need for a godly life through our knowledge of him who called us by his own glory and goodness"* (2 Peter 1:3 NIV). Through knowing and growing a relationship with God, you begin to discover why you were created, what has been put inside of you that can produce great wealth. Outside God, we cannot make true wealth because Deuteronomy 8:18 says, *"For it is He who is giving you power to make wealth"* (AMP). Having money is not wealth. But walking with God, discovering our purpose or calling, brings true wealth along with joy, peace, favor, and blessings. I know many do not agree with me on this, but that is the true life. Our children must be taught to use their gifts and talents as they grow their relationship with God to glorify Him in all they do. The Bible says; *"So whether you eat or drink or whatever you do, do it all for the glory of God"* (1 Corinthians 10:31 NIV).

It's so important to teach our children that the beginning and end of true wealth and financial freedom comes only from God. They may get the whole world but lose their soul if they fail to reconnect and use all that God has put in them for His glory. *"For what shall it profit a man, if he shall gain the whole world, and lose his own soul?"* (Mark 8:36 KJV). They must understand that the enemy is a thief; who only wants to destroy. John 10:10 (NIV) tells us, *"The thief comes only to steal and kill and destroy; I have come that they may have life and have it to the full."* Let them know that when they serve God with their gifts and talents, He will give them life in full on all sides. Serving God with their gifts and talents is not just serving in church, but using their gifts and talents in ways that will glorify God wherever they find themselves.

"Remember that your real wealth can be measured not by what you have, but by what you are."

—Napoleon Hill[16]

Teach Your Children How to Protect Their Mind: Here is a quote by Ernest Agyemang Yeboah, it says; "Even a computer guards itself against viruses, why not you? Guard your mind!" The Bible in Proverbs 4:23 (NIV) says; *"Above all else, guard your heart, for everything you do flows from it."*

Yes, it is important to teach our children to guard their hearts above everything else because our minds are like a hard drive. What we put in is what will come out of it. What you invest in your mind is what you will attract. Our children must understand that what they read, watch, and listen to determines their mental health. Most importantly, let them know they have the power to control what they feed their minds with.

The Bible encourages us on this in Philippians 4:8–9 (NIV):

> *Finally, brothers and sisters, whatever is true, whatever is noble, whatever is right, whatever is pure, whatever is lovely, whatever is admirable—if anything is excellent or praiseworthy—think about such things.*

If what they read, watch, and listen to does not match up with Philippians 4:8–9, then its negative, do not give it access to your mind nor dwell on it. See it for what it is; a virus aiming to harm and even destroy, leading to mental health issues. We must teach them to protect their minds, even from things that seem good.

No matter what we do, each instant contains infinite choices. What we choose to think about, say, or listen to creates what we momentarily feel. It conditions the quality of our communication and, in the end, the quality of our everyday life too.

Teach Them the Importance and Dangers of Social Media, Screens, and Gadgets. Our lives as we know it is greatly influenced by the internet. It has become part of our lives, and it is expedient to discuss its usage with our children, especially the older ones. It is wise and highly essential to painstakingly teach our children about this. When having a conversation about social media, it is important to anchor our teaching on Ephesians 4:29 (NIV): *"Do not let any unwholesome talk come out of your mouths, but only what is helpful for building others up according to their needs, that it may benefit those who listen."* This scripture will draw their attention to focus on only glorifying God and edifying others through their social media engagements.

Let them know to make their engagement on social media edifying. They need to know not to follow the scores of people on social media whose contents are glamorous and fake; aimed at being deceitful while leading many into depression. Let them know the foolishness of comparing themselves with what they see on social media. 2 Corinthians 10:12 (NIV) states that it's not wise to do that; This Bible verse says; *"when they measure themselves by themselves and compare themselves with themselves, they are not wise."*

It is important to teach our children how to spend time on their gadgets.

There are lots of health and social damages that can occur with the excessive use of gadgets and screen time. We must talk to children about these and set boundaries that can help them stay disciplined. Significant research has shown the negative effect of technology to a child's brain. Technology gives our children access to lots of information; it gives them the impression that the world is right in their palms, but it is also a child killer. It is important for children to experience their childhood because it comes only once in a lifetime. Many researches has shown that children learn more when they play with each other, run, jump, use their imaginations, read books, and dance. But we now have children who are addicted to their screens and gadgets, forever tapping and swiping mostly in isolation.

There are alarming results from research, and MRI scans that show that children who spend lots of hours on gadgets and screens playing video games and the lots, have same brains as people who are addicted to drugs!

Excessive use of gadgets and screen time, if not controlled, causes a huge damage to the development of the child's brain. This can affect their general health too, starting with depression, anxiety, low attention span, addiction, sleep deprivation, eye damage, social incompetence, excessive weight gain, and many more.

It is therefore wise to teach our children how to wisely manage their use of these gadgets and screen time. We can set limits on how long they can use it to help them develop and grow properly.

Here are some limits we can put in place to help our children grow and develop effectively:

- No screen in their rooms.

- Develop a daily routine that involve physical play with themselves or even with their toys and if possible, no screen time involved.
- Sleep time must be nine to eleven hours.
- Book reading;
- Physical sports (soccer, tennis, basketballball)
- Learning an instrument.
- Drawing
- Swimming
- Dance classes
- No gadget in the room during bedtime;
- Involve them in home chores, and
- If they must use gadgets and screens, it must be timed.

Teach Your Child How to Respect Themselves so They Can Respect Others: How to treat others with respect means knowing how to treat yourself with respect first. The Bible says in Mark 12:31 (NIV), *"The second is this: 'Love your neighbor as yourself.' There is no commandment greater than these."* Loving yourself is a sign of self-respect. And you cannot love others if you don't love yourself. Love is respect. If you don't respect yourself, you cannot respect others.

Loving yourself means knowing and appreciating who you are. When you acknowledge what God has done in your life, who you are in Him, (as one who is precious, bought with a price, loved by the almighty God, and known by Him), you will appreciate others because you will accord them the value you give to yourself.

Our children must understand this truth. They must work in this reality. It is our responsibility to teach them. Children must have self-love and self-respect in order for them to relate with others appropriately.

If our children fail to respect themselves, they will look to people to validate them. We should not forget that people have the ability to disappoint and fail others. We must teach our children to feel secure in the love of God that keeps them aware of who they truly are so they can love themselves and so that God's love will empower them to love and respect others around them.

> *"When our children walk with God, they will understand how to respect themselves because they will find their self-worth in God."*
>
> —Nene Oluwagbohun

CHAPTER 7

Teach Soft Skills

"The future belongs to those who learn more skills and combine them in creative ways."
—Robert Greene[17]

"People skills in leadership are not negotiable."
—Cristina Imre[18]

"A fool takes no pleasure in understanding, but only in expressing his opinion."
—Proverbs 18:2 (ESV)

"Common sense is not common."
—African Proverbs

Soft skills are essential for us and our children to continuously enjoy the blessings of God. God blesses us every day, but many people cannot enjoy the blessings of God because they do not have the soft skills required to enjoy them. The Bible says in Ephesian 1:3 (NIV), *"Praise be to the God and*

Father of our Lord Jesus Christ, who has blessed us in the heavenly realms with every spiritual blessing in Christ." This means God has blessed us all with all it takes to enjoy life. The question now however is, "do we have what it takes to receive and enjoy the blessings?"

In the design of life, God has His part to play, and you have your own part to play too. We cannot keep being religious by praying always and not teaching our children how to enjoy the blessings we are praying for. It would be a huge mess; if God blesses them, but they do not know how to enjoy the blessings because they lack the skills to help them tap into it. There are things God will not do for us, as we are expected to step up and do our part ourselves. God will not solve our problems for us, but He will provide the way out of those problems; as humans, we must be able to apply problem-solving skills to get issues resolved. God has placed people in our lives for us to bond, communicate and collaborate with for success and companionship.

Those intangible qualities that focus on behavior, personal traits, and brain-based skills (what we call common sense in Africa) are important in life today, more than ever, and we must be deliberate to teach our children these things. Without these skills, succeeding will be a far cry, irrespective of how spiritual they are.

Teach Your Children How to Make Decisions

As we raise our children, it is important to equip them with the information needed to help them make informed decisions. Teach your children how to make right choices. Because of the fall of man, life is governed by the law of cause and effects; good and bad; and then blessings and curses. But man has been given a greater ability and power to make choices. The choices we make determine if we will gain the rewards of making good choices or face the consequences of making bad (negative) choices.

Looking at how God, the originator of humans Himself treated the children of Israel as a family; we can glean a thing or two.. He spoke to Moses to teach the children of Israel how to make choices. He placed before them all the rewards and all the consequences that come as a result of their decision-making. Deuteronomy 30:19—31:1 (NIV) tells us what Moses said:

> *This day I call the heavens and the earth as witnesses against you that I have set before you life and death, blessings, and curses. Now choose life, so that you and your children may live and that you may love the LORD your God, listen to his voice, and hold fast to him. For the LORD is your life, and he will give you many years in the land he swore to give to your fathers, Abraham, Isaac and Jacob. . . . Then Moses went out and spoke these words to all Israel.*

This is a very important soft skill we must teach our children early because someday, our children will be independent, and the decisions they make will determine the results they will get. Let them know there are great consequences for choosing to do the wrong things, and there are blessings and great rewards for choosing to do right. We live in a world today where people believe *their* truth, but there is nothing as "their/my/our truth." It's either truth based on the principles laid out for life or no truth at all.

God speaking again in Deuteronomy 11:26–30 (NKJV):

> *Behold, I set before you today a blessing and a curse: the blessing, if you obey the commandments of the LORD your God which I command you today; and the curse, if you do not obey the commandments of the LORD your God, but turn aside from the way which I command you today, to go after other gods which you have not known.*

We must understand that this is how life is governed. Most of the blessings we enjoy today are based on the choices we have made, and most of the pain we suffer today is because of the choices we also made. Empowering, encouraging and guiding our children early to make their decision is very important. This does not mean they will not make mistakes; they definitely will. I mean, just like babies stumble, fall and graze their knees while learning to walk, but keep at it till they become competent, they will fall making choices. The key thing is to stagger back up, learn lessons from the bad decisions and move forward.

Don't be afraid of their falling; they will fall even if you became a physical shield. You may warn, advice and guide them away from mistakes but don't protect them from making the mistakes. It will give you the opportunity to reaffirm what you have been teaching, and give them the opportunity to be a part of the training and learning process.

Training a child comes with hands-on practice as we give them room to make those decisions. Again, don't forget they will fall, and make mistakes, but don't feel discouraged or frustrated. I always advise parents not to set expectations on children while teaching them; rather, set expectations for yourself not to give up. Make a decision to go through the process of training and learning, knowing that they will understand and appreciate you deeply someday. That is the nature of true love. God never gives up on us, so never give up on your children. Your patience with them will make them confident adults in the future.

Teach Your Children How to Be Clean and Be Involved with Household Chores

It is important to teach children early how to do house chores and to take care of their personal hygiene. Teaching your children this helps them stay neat, healthy and organized. It's important to start by giving them age-appropriate chores.

Make a checklist to keep you organized and to help you track their progress with their assigned chores.

Let your children know house chores are not just a must-do or an important pathway to self-sufficiency but their responsibility and contribution to the family as legitimate members. Reiterate that chores give them the vital opportunity to practice how to care for their own space and demonstrate their sense of ownership for your beautiful family.

> "Clean and organized is a practice, not a project."
> —Meagan Francis[19]

Dear parents, it's very important to verbally commend your children when they do a good job, and encourage them to try again when they do not do such a fantastic job.

When it comes to correcting your children regarding undone or poorly done chores, it's important to correct them in love. Patiently go over the chores again for them to see how it's done, then let them try it themselves while you supervise. This will enhance their willingness to learn and to be teachable.

Teach Your Children about Taking Up Responsibilities.

Responsibility is simply being accountable. True leaders take responsibility. A family is a team, and every team member must have a role to play to achieve the set goals of the family.

For instance, if one of our family goals is to have a clean home, everyone should be responsible for that.

In a family, everyone should have their responsibilities. Yes! We all have responsibilities; the parent's responsibility is to provide and pay the bills. The children are responsible for doing the chores. If our children understand that their chores are not just mere duties but responsibilities, it would help them understand the importance of teamwork and become more effective wherever they find themselves.

I always say to my sons, if I fail to provide for the family, I have failed in my responsibility. And if you fail to fix up the house, wash the dishes, fix your room, and all, you have failed in your responsibilities. So when a guest comes in and finds our house looking unkempt, you are responsible for that, just as I am responsible for the electricity that was cut off because I failed to do mine.

Taking responsibility and learning to be accountable at home has a long-lasting, healthy effect on children, because ultimately, it makes them responsible leaders and awesome teammates at work. They also do not need to be coaxed or courted to do their part in a team because they understand right away why it is important for everyone to play their respective roles. Remember this, Winston Churchill once said, *"The price of greatness is responsibility."*[20]

Teach Your Children How to Set Boundaries and Respect Others

Setting boundaries is very important for everyone, especially when relating with other people. Unfortunately, not everyone understands boundary setting.

It does not matter if people understand this or not; what is important is that we respect boundaries. It is therefore paramount that our children need to learn it early in life.

It's not just okay to teach children how to set boundaries, it's also important to teach them to respect other people's boundaries too. Doreen Virtue puts it this way: *"Boundaries are a part of self-care. They are healthy, normal, and necessary."*

Boundaries are simply necessary and very healthy; they show people how you want to be treated. This is very needful for healthy and lasting relationships.

This could mean telling someone to stop calling you a particular nickname or simply correcting someone who pronounced your name wrongly. It could also mean telling someone you like the way they treat you and showing them the way you want to be treated. Someone rightly said this: *"lack of boundaries invites lack of respect."*

Teaching children this skill will help them build their self-confidence as well as, great, and lasting relationships with others as they grow.

Here Are Some Ways You Can Help Your Children Set Boundaries.

- Ensure they know who they are.
- Ensure they know what they want and how they want to be treated.
- Encourage them to firmly insist on how they want to be treated.
- Teach them to avoid using "maybe" or "I think" when expressing their thoughts because it makes them look unsure and their message unclear.
- Encourage them to respectfully say "No" to things they do not want.
- Encourage your children to speak up when people ignore their set boundaries and keep treating them the way they do not like.
- Ensure to set boundaries around them, too, and make sure they are respecting your boundaries. By so doing, they will respect other people's boundaries around them.

Teach Your Children How to Have Healthy, Balanced Self-esteem and Gratitude

A healthy and balanced self-esteem starts with a rich mindset about yourself. Harvey Fierstein puts it this way: *"Never be bullied into silence. Never allow yourself to be made a victim. Accept no one's definition of your life, but define yourself."* Our children must never allow themselves to be victims of circumstances. They need to remember that they are unique, beautiful and made in God's image. That they are saved, redeemed, and set free by God and so, he does not remember what they used to be like before they got saved. Hebrews 12:8 (NIV) puts it like this: *"For I will forgive their wickedness and will remember their sins no more."* John 8:36 concludes this line of thought with; *"So if the Son makes you free, then you are unquestionably free"* (AMP).

We must teach our children to discover themselves in God as we teach them about who He is and what He has done on the cross to set them free. Let them understand why they must believe in their hearts that Christ died for them and confess with their mouths to be saved and set free. Romans 10:9 (NIV) says, *"If you declare with your mouth, 'Jesus is Lord,' and believe in your heart that God raised him from the dead, you will be saved."*

Every child needs to know and do this to reconnect with their Father. This is at the point they finally find themselves and define who they are. They cannot define themselves outside God. Money, gifts, toys, and games cannot define who they are; only God can define them explicitly. He calls them His image, His product, the creation of His hands. He is the manufacturer and one can only find meaning in Him as His products.

What an awesome privilege to know the manufacturer one on one! The children will truly come to understand more about the value and the usefulness of them being products of God, Hallelujah! Knowing who they are will keep them solidly away from pride. Instead, they will be filled with confidence in God and gratitude for His gift.

Eleanor Roosevelt once said: *"No one can make you feel inferior without your consent."* This is where their confidence is: knowing who and whose they are. Our children must be confident to declare Hebrews 13:6 (NKJV): *"So we say with confidence, 'The Lord is my helper; I will not be afraid. What can mere mortals do to me?'"*

We must teach them to always be grateful. Yes, gratitude is a skill they must learn. David said in Psalm 9:1 (NIV): *"I will give thanks to you, Lord, with all my heart; I will tell of all your wonderful deeds."* One of the best things about gratitude is that it's a choice you must make; the more you choose to do it, the easier it becomes. The more you profess gratitude, the more you find more things to be grateful for. Will Arnett says this about gratitude: *"I am happy because I'm grateful. I choose to be grateful. That gratitude allows me to be happy."* If you want your children to be happy, teach them to show gratitude always to God and those around them.

When we navigate our children to a place of having healthy and balanced self-esteem; and a confident and grateful outlook to life, their life becomes wholesome, complete and well-rounded. It will reflect in how they respect themselves and others. They will not be proud, nor will they live in a bubble, expecting the world to revolve around them. Instead, they will be kind with their words and deeds, charitable, empathetic, good mannered, and have an attitude that esteems God.

Teach Your Children the Act of Asking and Sharing

> *"Take the risk to ask for whatever you need and want. If someone says no, you will not lose anything. If someone says yes, you have a lot to gain."*
>
> —Abhishek Ratna[21]

Asking for permission is a soft skill we must teach our children. Asking for permission shows you respect people and their possessions. It's not a big deal to get a "no" when you ask for a favor or something; you will not lose anything. Children must be taught to respect people's possession, not just people outside the family, but also within the immediate family. Let them know that, to use something that isn't theirs, they must ask for it before taking it. This does not just involve asking, but they must have the permission to go ahead.

As a professional, I have seen lots of children take people's things without asking, especially in school. Unfortunately, they were labeled thieves. This isn't a good place for a child because it can destroy a child's self-confidence. But when we teach them to ask first before taking or using someone else's possession, they will be able to apply it in school, at work, and even when they get married.

While we teach them to ask, we must teach them how to share. It's important to encourage them to share their possession, especially when they are not using them. Amazingly, sharing has a lot of health benefits because when people share or experience gratitude from the person they shared with, they experience the release of a hormone known as oxytocin from the brain. This is the hormone responsible for relieving stress and improving the immune function in people. Sharing makes people happy and builds social interactions.

Teach Your Children Effective Communication:

In teaching children effective communication, it is important to teach them that their views are important, and that other's views are also equally important. *Having* great communication skills and knowing how to deploy this skill will help them in their careers and relationship with others. In this age where children are easily distracted, teaching children to pay attention to and understanding nonverbal cues, will help them notice their environment when communication is going on. It may save them from wicked and unscrupulous criminals too.

When teaching children effective communication, it is important to teach them how to use kind words and respectful vocabularies like: **Please, thank you, I am sorry, may I,** and **can I?** In Colossian 4:6 (NIV) the Bible says we should speak with grace: *"Let your conversation be always full of grace, seasoned with salt, so that you may know how to answer everyone."*

Salt preserves; salt puts taste to the food. When our children speak respectfully and kindly, their words becomes an encouragement to many people. John Powell has this to say about communication, he said: *"Communication works for those who work at it."* Teaching children effective communication from home like how to listen, take turns to speak, use kind words, and respectful vocabularies will help them thrive in life.

Teach Your Children Problem-solving:

Roger Lewin said this: *"Too often we give our children answers to remember rather than problems to solve."* This statement is so true. It is important as parent to remember that problems are part of life. If we are humans, we will have problems from time to time, and our children are not exempted from the problems and challenges of life. Instead of solving or giving them answers to these problems, they can be guided on how to handle them. Our job as parents is to equip them with the "how to". Teaching them this skill will help them navigate through life to grow healthy relationships and stay mentally healthy.

Philippians 4:13 (NIV) tells us, "*I can do all things through Christ which strengthened me.*" Because they have Christ in them, they can solve any problem. They have the Holy Spirit who can show, teach and remind them all things you have taught them too. He also gives them the wisdom on how to handle life issues; All they need to do is partner with Him.

Problem-solving skills can help children deal with depression as they grow. We must engage them to take responsibility for their actions and choices by asking open-ended questions that make them think and come up with solutions to the challenge at hand. This will help build their resilience so they will not give up easily when faced with challenges, but rather, would think through and come up with alternative solution to their problems.

Here are some steps we can teach our children to follow as they solve problems:

- Encourage them to identity the problem: just like naming or calling out emotions they feel at a time; this

will enable them think through on how to resolve the problem.
- Encourage them to think through several options of solutions; this will activate their creative juices and remind them to depend on the Holy Spirit for help.
- Ask them questions about the possible consequences for each solution they come up with; this will always help them think through the consequences for each potential solution and discern which to choose.
- After their careful consideration of the consequences to each solution, encourage them to pick a solution.

Teach Your Children Resilience and How to Overcome Failure:

In building resilience and helping children overcome failure, I believe so much in what Dieter F. Uchtdorf said: *"It's your reaction to adversity, not adversity itself that determines how your life's story will develop."*[22] We must teach our children to never give up but try again and again. Avoid helping them resolve their problems and challenges.

We must let them understand that even when we are not physically present with them, they are never alone. Let us stand back and trust God to help them make wise choices. It is said that, *"Tough times never last, but tough people do."* As they interact with other children, they will develop the grit they need to go through life whenever they have roadblocks or challenges.

Psychologists say that children who engage in all the activities mentioned here have less risk of getting into destructive behaviors or even being depressed. In the end, rest in knowing that God is with them as he was with Joshua in Joshua 1:9: *"I repeat, be strong and brave! Don't be afraid and don't panic, for I, the LORD your God, am with you in all you do"* (NKJV).

I will strongly encourage you to make Habakkuk 3:17–18 (NKJV) their confession:

> *Even though the fig trees have no blossoms, and there are no grapes on the vines; even though the olive crop fails, and the fields lie empty and barren; even though the flocks die in the fields, and the cattle barns are empty, yet I will rejoice in the Lord! I will be joyful in the God of my salvation!*

Teach Your Children Forgiveness:

There is a quote that says, *"Holding a grudge doesn't make you strong, it makes you bitter. Forgiving doesn't make you weak, it sets you free."* This quote is amazing. Forgiveness is a gift, and we must give it to our children willingly. When we forgive our children, we give them a great opportunity to understand the forgiveness of God. Never hold back forgiveness from your children; forgive and forget it. Don't revisit the incident again but rather give them the freedom to learn from their mistake without guilt.

Whenever we revisit our children's past or wrongdoings, we increase their guilt consciousness, something they are already dealing with, instigated by the enemy of their soul. The Bible calls him the accuser of the brethren in Revelation 12:10: "*for the accuser of our brethren is cast down, who accused them before our God day and night*" (ASV). But when our children enjoy forgiveness from us, they grow confident to embrace the forgiveness of God while overcoming the lies and accusations of the devil over them.

When our children learn forgiveness from us, it becomes easier to give forgiveness to others without holding back and carrying unforgiveness about, which could have adverse effect to their wellbeing.

CHAPTER 8

Be a Great Friend

"I learned that a real friendship is not about what you can get, but what you can give. Real friendship is about making sacrifices and investing in people to help them improve their lives."
—Eric Thomas[23]

"A man who has friends must himself be friendly, But there is a friend who sticks closer than a brother."
—Proverbs 18:24 (NKJV)

True friendship is a gift from God. When we have friends in our lives, it gives us a sense of belonging, increases our confidence, and helps us reduce stress. We never feel alone especially during tough times because of the support we get from them. Scientists have revealed that people who have healthy friendship networks (people who share same values with you) are less likely to have mental health issues and high blood pressure because those friendships make it easier to avoid unhealthy lifestyles. People in such circles tend to have prolonged lives.

Cultivating strong and healthy friendships have become a huge challenge in our tech society today. There is therefore a need to teach social skills to help our preteens who will grow into teenagers eager for true friends outside their immediate family. It's not that easy to find such true friendship or relationships on phones and tablets.

There is a need for human interactions, and no video game can exactly replace human beings because, humans are designed to interact with one another. This means that socials skills must be practiced in real life, in homes where parents model healthy relationships to their children. Sadly, there has been a drastic shift with the use of the phones and tablets in our homes, which makes everyone absent as they seem present, but in the real sense, they are all glued to their gadgets. This has terribly corroded relationships between spouses, parents and their children.

Technology is good but also has its negative effects on human relationships. In my career as a speaker, I have heard alarming questions from families who are disturbed by the dazzling amount of time spouses and children spend on their gadgets. Children are fixated on their phones or games instead of getting involved to build great memories. Memories of playing with other kids in the backyard, riding bicycles, playing boardgames, eating lunches and doing their home chores. They struggle to play board games, finish their school homework, sustain conversations, and even eat their meals without being distracted because they are itching to get back to their game or their phones.

There are lots of disturbing statistics that shows the amount of time people; especially children spend on technology. It's disturbing because these children end up being influenced by opinions that are wrong, untrue or half-truth. Many parents have gone a step further to introduce their children to social media platforms like TikTok, Instagram, and others without realizing the dangers or ripple effect the use of these platforms can have on these children. For instance, for most people, when social media expectations are not met, it always results to depression, anxiety, and anger in adults and this could be worse for children who have not built capacity process and declutter their thoughts. This will have a negative effect on their general social skills, its best to wait for them to mature first.

Children need real relationships to grow their identities and confidence, and parents are naturally positioned to affirm this. I have heard parents say they are afraid of their children making friends because of peer pressure, to solve this dilemma, they keep them indoors. As much as that is understandable, especially considering the times and age we are in, our children need to interact with others, as we help our children, we can deliberately become family friends- with people who share the same family values with us, whose children are growing with our children in same age range. This is a great way to model friendship.

This relationship can be positioned to teach and model good values, show them their worth, teach them to prioritize, and the principles that govern their lives. If they understand these things early, it would help them choose good friends. It would also position them to positively influence people around them. We cannot always choose who should, can be or not be their friends, especially in school, but the values and principles we have taught them, will be a guide to them as they choose their friends wisely.

Some parent resort to prayer only, but while prayer is perfect, teaching them the right thing to do will bring a great balance. Here are some of the most important things children should be taught and must understand about friendships as they grow.

- They must understand their value.
- We must teach them how to be authentic and honest.
- Teach them how to appreciate other people's differences, respect their opinions and ideals, and not judge or be manipulative.
- They must learn the act of listening to others when engaged in a conversation.
- The act of receiving feedback from others without feeling hurt is very important.

- We must teach them that every relationship goes through its seasons, and conflict is one of them.
- We must teach them how to use the golden words: "Please" when asking for something; "I am sorry," (when they hurt people; to show remorse, sympathy) and "thank you" to show appreciation.
- We must teach the importance of forgiveness when they are hurt in a relationship.
- We must teach our children how to compliment others and how to receive compliments by modeling it to them at home.
- We must teach our children how to be involved in healthy competition.
- We must teach our children the important of trust in a relationship.

As we model friendship to our children, our children learn a lot and absorb just by mere watching and observing.

Through the model of friendship we have deliberately built, our children will observe different dynamics of friendship, like knowing how to resolve conflicts when they are among friends and understanding when to let a friendship go if it is no longer serving its purpose without being hurt because not all friendships will last forever.

Children also learn empathy- the ability to connect with people by understanding and sharing in their feelings through friendships. We live in a me-centered world today, and not us-centered, and this has made it very difficult to connect with people. The Bible calls it signs of the last days. Self-centeredness is the spirit of the last days. 2 Timothy 3:1–5 (KJV) warns us: *"This know also, that in the last days perilous times shall come. 2 For men shall be lovers of their own selves, covetous, boasters, proud, blasphemers, disobedient to parents, unthankful, unholy, 3 Without natural affection."* We must help our children to live above this season.

When our children build and establish good, trusted friendships with people around, they grow mentally strong and healthy; enjoy lower rates of anxiety; have higher-functioning immune systems and share a more optimistic outlook in life; their emotions are well-regulated; they are happier, more empathetic, and able to stay connected to people.

CHAPTER 9

Instructing

"A mind without instruction cannot bear fruit than can a field however be fertile, without cultivation."
—*Marcus Tullius Cicero*[24]

"A wise person will listen and take in more instruction."
—*Solomon*[25]

"Hear, my son, your father's instruction, and forsake not your mother's teaching."
—*Proverbs 1:8(NIV)*

Being instructive as a parent means to educate, help, illuminate, and enlighten your children with the information you have, to guide them into becoming better individuals. The Bible in Proverbs 1:8 (NIV) calls you an instructor because you have lived long enough and gained experiences that have positioned you to lead your children with their best interest at heart. *"Hear, my son, your father's instruction, and forsake not your mother's teaching."* One in authority is expected to give instructions, but many parents have relinquished their position to their children who tend to be the ones giving the instructions in the home, and this practice is not healthy for the child or the society in any way.

Some parents have failed to take their place of leadership, hence allowing children manipulate and push them around.

Leadership is not a title; it's a position accompanied with lots of responsibilities and commitments, and one of this responsibility is to instruct. The Merriam Dictionary says to instruct means; "to provide with authority information, commands, and directives."

Giving our children instructions is likened to giving your children precious jewel. Proverbs 1:9 explains what instruction looks like on every child, it says; *"They are a garland to grace your head and a chain to adorn your neck"* (NIV). If you want your child to look great and amazing with the garland of grace on their head and chains that adorn their necks, give them instructions. This means when our children practice how to follow instructions from home, they will be well admired and respected everywhere they go.

Marcus Tullius Cicero says, *"A mind without instruction cannot bear fruit."*[24] There are instructions everywhere you go. You find them in the stores, on the streets, at school, in the gym, at the doctor's office, in the Word of God, just about everywhere!

Instructions are designed to protect and lead us. Once a child understands how to obey instructions from home, it becomes easier to obey God's instructions.

As a matter of fact, every little child wants to be instructed by their parents. They desperately need their parents to give them direction and leadership. This is why they sometimes end up disrespecting their parents if they sense a lack of leadership. A child feels safe when you give instructions and lead well. Leadership gives them bearing. It is very important to know that this stage of parenting is only for a very short time because there also comes a season when they do not want to be instructed but rather supported. We will look at that in the next chapter.

Would you say after the teaching is done, then comes the stage of instruction? I am inclined to say no to that because instructing children is another level of teaching a child. It is a stage where children are instructed to carry out what they have been taught. For instance, after examples of solving a math problem are taught, the student is then instructed to use those examples that were taught to solve new problems. This example also applies to teaching children how to make their beds and letting them make it after. It's important to always instruct them to take ownership of, and responsibility for lessons learned to apply them in their lives.

This stage of parenting is also very sensitive as children are very observant. They observe how you are modeling what you are instructing them to do. If you are instructing them to read books and not spend excessive time playing games, the question is, are you also reading, or you are always watching TV or playing games? The truth is, you cannot be effective in this stage of parenting without living an exemplary life. Not practicing what you are instructing them to do is very unrealistic.

When you ask your children to be respectful to people, but you are not respectful to people in your life and around you, you are wrong. Children are always watching, so we must be deliberate about our behavior around them. Because you are human and prone to making mistakes, if you find that you have broken rules around them, it's important to have a conversation with your children about it. Apologize if you need to, and tell them how you will handle that kind of situation the next time.

In this stage of instructing, rules must be set, and the consequences of disobeying them must be set too. The reason for setting rules is because rules provide emotional and physical safety to a child unless they disobey, then they face the consequences. Rules in the family help children understand boundaries. This is not because the child is a bad child or ill behaved, but because children sometimes naturally act mischievous or manipulative. Children will sometimes misbehave just to test your limits, to determine if you are still in control, or find out if you are still leading. Be mindful of how you react or respond because your responses speak a lot at this point.

When children lose confidence or feel unsafe with your leadership, it leads to anxiety and fear. They become fearful of the unknown, because even though they are full of mischief, children are designed to follow instructions. To maintain leadership, be firm with your rules. Let them face the rewards or consequences of breaking the rules.

Rules should be set in a way that children fully comprehend what is being taught. The instructions are derived from the teaching to help track of how the children are engaging with the teaching. When they break the rules or fail to follow the instructions, it is a great time to revisit and reinforce the teaching. One of the measures used when rules are broken is called discipline. Discipline helps to enforce the teaching.

Discipline is not about punitive punishment; rather, it is ensuring that children understand the law of cause and effect; that there are consequences for every action in life. Some parents believe discipline is not necessary. This belief is very unhealthy, and it has negative effect on children's social skills. Parenting without discipline is a destructive way of raising children. One of the proofs of true love is discipline. Even God disciplines His children, and children have great respect for the parent who disciplines them. Hebrews 12:4–11 (MSG) tells us:

In this all-out match against sin, others have suffered far worse than you, to say nothing of what Jesus went through—all that bloodshed! So don't feel sorry for yourselves. Or have you forgotten how good parents treat children, and that God regards you as his children?

My dear child, don't shrug off God's discipline, but don't be crushed by it either.

It's the child he loves that he disciplines; the child he embraces, he also corrects.

God is educating you; that's why you must never drop out. He's treating you as dear children. This trouble you're in isn't punishment; it's training, the normal experience of children. **Only irresponsible parents leave children to fend for themselves. Would you prefer an irresponsible God? We respect our own parents for training and not spoiling us, so why not embrace God's training so we can truly live?** *While we were children, our parents did what seemed best to them. But God is doing what is best for us, training us to live His holy best. At the time, discipline isn't much fun. It always feels like it's going against the grain. Later, of course, it pays off big-time, for it's the well-trained who find themselves mature in their relationship with God.*

Proverbs 3:12 (NIV) says, "because the Lord disciplines those he loves, as a father the son he delights in."

True love makes us delight in our children, and if we delight in them, we will discipline them. Lack of discipline in parenting reveals a lack of true love. To leave a child all to themselves without discipline is having a child grow like a wild plant without control, prone to hurting everyone and even themselves. The Bible instructs us not to withhold discipline from our children. Proverbs 23:13 (NIV) says, *"Do not withhold discipline from a child;"* If God, the one who initiated parenting, disciplines His children because He loves them, this then reveals to us that discipline is important and cannot be done without love. Don't forget God Himself is love personified. First John 4:8 (NIV) states, *"Anyone who does not love does not know God, because God is love."*

I totally understand why a lot of parents are uncomfortable about disciplining their children because of how their folks disciplined them as children. As much as your experience is real, it does not rule out the need to discipline your children, especially considering the great benefits to your children and the society at large.

I suggest that you pause and look back at the circumstances that surrounded you discipline experiences as a growing child as you we move on:

Lots of parents did not know any better; they disciplined us the best way they knew how. Hebrews 12:10 (NLT) states that *"For our earthly fathers disciplined us for a few years, doing the best they knew how."*

- Parents were going through lots of frustration.
- Many had anger issues that they had not dwelt with.
- Many even had mental health issues that they were not even aware of.
- And many meant well but never knew how to do it right.

I would like to encourage you not to dwell on the hurt, but rather consider this list above and forgive them, just as Christ said on the cross, in Luke 23:34 *"Father, forgive them, for they do not know what they are doing."* Forgive them so you can be free to follow the pattern laid down by God for parenting.

We cannot rule out discipline in parenting because it's one of the parenting patterns God laid for parenting. The Bible states the importance of discipline in Proverbs 19:18 (ESV): *"Discipline your son, for there is hope; do not set your heart on putting him to death."* If we fail to discipline our children, we are leaving them to be destroyed by the enemy.

Another reason why some parents do not want to discipline their children is because they do not want to make their children angry or sad, and perhaps to avoid conflicts. Disciplining your child may cause conflict or make them angry with you momentarily but focus on the benefits in the future. The end result of the discipline will be of great benefit to them and everyone. Your children will someday appreciate and respect you because you disciplined them. Hebrews 12:6 (MSG) says, *"We respect our own parents for training and not spoiling us."*

The Bible explains this in Hebrews 12:11 (ESV) *"For the moment all discipline seems painful rather than pleasant, but later it yields the peaceful fruit of righteousness to those who have been trained by it."*

Lots of parents fail to discipline their children because they want to be friends with their children. Dear parent, your child is not your friend, especially at this stage. Your role is to be a parent, not to be a friend. It is too much responsibility to place on the child to carry. Sharing secrets with your child or having adult talks with them is not psychologically, emotionally, or spiritually healthy for that child.

When friendship with your child is what drives your parenting, you will always feel guilty for disciplining your child, thereby, losing your position as a parent, and leaving the child without guidance and protection. It's important to take up your responsibility as a parent and deal with the guilt, no matter how you feel.

Instead of feeling guilty and destroying your child's life, be present in their lives by setting your priorities straight, and making time for your children. Take them out and watch movies together, go on vacations together, read books together, and have conversations with them to bond strongly. This way, when the need for discipline arises, you would correct without feeling guilty. There would be no confusion whatsoever that they are loved and safely nestled in your leadership. This is a great way to get rid of guilt and to consistently remind yourself that children need discipline to be healthy and become responsible individuals.

Some parents are too lazy to discipline so they make excuses that the children are stressed and allow them to misbehave. Always remember that children sometimes test your limits. It is important to address misbehavior on time so it doesn't send the wrong message to the child that it's okay or you are not a good enough leader. It is paramount that you establish and demonstrate your ability to lead. Discipline makes our children feel safe, and we must find healthy ways to engage in disciplining them.

Positive and Negative Discipline

In engaging in discipline, be intentional to use positive discipline, not negative discipline. There are two types of disciplines: Negative discipline is an unhealthy way of disciplining a child, and this type could be very destructive. This is a discipline, fueled with anger and pain. We see this type of discipline when parents consistently yell and use abusive words in their interactions with their children. Some go as far as calling them names, which then makes them feel small, unworthy and undermined. We must know that anger does not go well with disciplining a child.

It is important to cool off from your anger before disciplining your child.

Disciplining in anger is like driving under an influence of a substance. Calm is the key. Disciplining in anger never gives you the opportunity to correct objectively. You end up doing or saying things that scar the child emotionally. You will definitely end up in regrets. After an anger bout, some parents apologize for being unreasonable or cruel but most parents who discipline like this do not even apologize because of their pride. That confuses the child. They become unsure of where they stand with you, if they should trust you or not. This is emotional insecurity.

Many of us have made this error while disciplining our children. It's not too late; we can repent and have a change of heart to do right by our children. Next, be willing and ready to apologize if you make the mistake again.

Here are some of the habits you would want to avoid while disciplining your children and the right attitude to adopt.

- When disciplining a child, focus on the now; don't go over their past mistakes. Let their past be their past, while you concentrate on the now, with the focus and hope that they will change. God never remembers our past mistakes. It's important to never bring an old account back so our children don't squirm in guilt instead of feeling redeemed.

- Don't discipline your child in anger; rather, take a walk or breathe if you are angry before handling that situation.

- When disciplining your child, don't label them. Do not call them by the name of the mistake or by the error that just happened. For instance: if your child took someone's pen without asking for permission, do not label them a thief. Rather deal with the issues by having a conversation about disrespecting people's boundaries and privacy, to reinforce that teaching again. Let them understand the consequences of their actions by choosing one of the disciplinary measures you both lay out for correction. Some parenting experts say this is lecturing a child. As much as it may sound like lecturing a child, it is the best thing to do at that moment, and I assure you they are listening. While still in that conversation, ask open-ended questions and navigate the conversation to where they can take responsibility for their actions.

- Do not shout or yell at your child when you want to discipline them, and don't use condescending words on them too. It is disrespectful. Rather, ask genuine questions that will help you both find the root of that behavior. Ask questions like; "Why did you do that? What were you thinking when you were doing that? How do you feel now that you are here?" This will bring up conversations that will lead to setting agreeable consequences. You must be firm while doing that.

- Never think of discipline as disrespecting your children, they are not synonymous. Rather see it as a means to reaffirm what you have been teaching. Let them always understand the disciplinary measure you are taking, whether they agree or not. There has to be a consequence for the behavior they exhibited. Be firm about the consequences always.

"Fathers, do not provoke your children to anger by the way you treat them. Rather, bring them up with the discipline and instruction that comes from the Lord" (Eph. 6:4 NLT).

Everyone wants to be treated with respect, even your child no matter how young they are, they understand when they are disrespected. We must ensure to respect them even as we discipline them in love. Love they say *"covers the multitude of sins"* 1 Peter 4:8 (NIV) this includes our errors that they enemy may want to manipulate and provoke our children with.

The second kind of discipline is Positive discipline is a discipline approached deliberately in an emotionally balanced environment state. Positive discipline is done with the intention to build, correct, impact, teach, encourage and lead the child to do, and become a better person. This helps them make good choices and stay in control of their behavior.

Positive discipline is partnering and depending on God to help and give us the wisdom to always say the right words, do or take the right actions and know how best to approach the incident at hand.

There are lots of benefits to disciplining children from a conscious and balanced state of emotions.

- At this state, you are calm and can think more objectively.
- You are more positive when correcting the child,
- You set an example of a positive and healthy tradition for your children to learn and follow in how to discipline others.
- We express the love of God through positive discipline,
- We express redemption through positive discipline.
- With positive discipline we treat our children with respect,
- We empower our children with courage to become better individuals.
- We demonstrate to our children that we trust them.

- Positive discipline gives us the opportunity to teach and instruct again.

Just as healthy food is to the body, discipline is very important for the well-rounded development of every child. It is necessary for their happiness and well-being because it helps them navigate through life's challenges.

When we use discipline as a part of our parenting practice, we will enjoy rest. Proverbs 29:17 (ESV) explains this also, it says: *"Discipline your son, and he will give you rest; he will give delight to your heart."*

Discipline is not designed to be pleasurable. Discipline is not for the now; it's for the future. Think of the rest, the peace, the joy, and the benefits of raising a well-disciplined child, and actively engage in the act of disciplining your child.

Let's talk about instructing children...

There are fun and great ways to give instructions to your children. Many parents today are failing to give their children instructions. Lots of children do not know how to obey instructions because parent don't give instructions; instead they go ahead to do it for them, which is not good for your child. Instructions are designed for our good; to direct, lead, protect, and make us wise; to make wise decisions.

How to give instructions:

- Don't give a child instruction on things you have not taught them. (Teaching builds connections for instruction.)
- Be firm with your instruction.
- Give age-appropriate instructions.
- Be specific with your instruction, for instance; say, "Do not move from the table to the kitchen."
- Don't give many instructions at one time; give one instruction at a time.
- When giving an instruction, be sure the child heard you; if possible, let them repeat the instruction back to you.
- Speak quietly and softly when giving a child instruction; it gets their attention.

CHAPTER 10

Coaching

"The interesting thing about coaching is that you have to trouble the comfortable and comfort the troubled."
—Ric Charlesworth[26]

"Coaching focuses on equipping the individual to discover their unique potential."
—Brian Cagneey[27]

"A life coach does for the rest of your life what a personal trainer does for your health and fitness."
—Elaine MacDonald[28]

"Train up a child in the way he should go; even when he is old he will not depart from it."
—Proverbs 22:6 (ESV)

I always say training is a process of learning that equips people to function in life and this process is a lifetime process that goes through different stages. According to Family development

theories, the family life circle has two major stages—expansion and contraction stage. The expansion stages are seasons when children are born and raised.
—Duvall 1957[29]

At this stage of parenting when coaching is needed, the goal of the parent is to support their children to navigate through this stage of autonomy and still share a wholesome bond with their children.

Someone may want to ask me if there is a difference between coaching and teaching and I would respond with; "There is a huge difference between the two."

In parenting, teaching is significantly the act of impacting knowledge and giving the child plenty opportunities to hone life skills. This process helps the child thrive. It gives the child a lot of spiritual, mental, social, and emotional capital. Please do not miss the teaching stage of parenting.

Coaching on the other hand is also a process of learning that leaves the children poised to take responsibility for their actions while you are in the background giving the needed supports and help. The act of coaching awakens the need for both the child and parent to work closely. It reminds the parent to earn their child's trust, stay committed to loving and supporting the child without judging them so they can grow into reasonable and responsible adults.

Teenage hood is the stage when children are becoming independent and so do not appreciate being bossed around or told what to do. The funny thing is, they still deeply desire a non-judgmental person who will be firm, forthright, and fair to coach and support them in this phase.

In this phase, you must hold your children accountable because they are practicing what you taught then over the years. Ask genuine questions and have meaningful conversations with them as often as possible and when there's need for it. Many teenagers may not want to talk about their thoughts or experiences but genuine connection will pave the way to build trust for even uncomfortable conversations. They will eventually open up when they sense your genuine need and curiosity to know and help. As long as you make your home a psychological safe environment, a no yelling zone, where they are free to speak and will not be judged, hushed or embarrassed, you will eventually bond with your teenager. Create one-on-one time with your teenager, have dinner or lunch, take walks or long drives together so you can connect to talk. This is a great way to connect with your teenager as you coach them.

Teenage hood is not the time to teach your children the ABC's of life. Rather it's their first internship; a time to practice what they have learnt so far. A lot of parents make this mistake; they do not begin the tutoring stage of the child's life early and try to play catch up when the children have become teenagers. That is wrong season, wrong timing. When we miss out during the formative stages of our children's lives, experiences have proven that it's always hard to steer and correct them at this stage. If we are not careful at this point, parent–child relationship gets strained.

In raising teenagers, you must learn to adjust your parenting style, avoid being bossy and controlling. The days of spanking and commanding are over at this stage, but rather hold the much needed conversations at this stage and earn their trust.

Lucy said to me, *"As a teenager, I feel very motivated and excited, knowing I have some people who trust and believe in me and those people are my number one teacher and influencers, they are the ones I have grown up to see and know, and today they are my number one fans. They are always cheering, supporting, coaching, and encouraging me so I can live out my beliefs and values to become all I am designed to be by my creator."*

At the stage when teenagers step up to be responsible for their actions, parent must become patient by stepping back to avoid being judgmental, because if you do, it could make them defensive or rebellious. We must understand that coaching deals with real-life experiences and challenges. Our teenagers are dealing with real-life experiences that make for bad decisions, especially because they are against the values you have instilled in them. They need someone to continuously affirm and remind them of the rules; someone to cheer them on to build their self-discipline skills too.

Let your coaching torch shine brightly so that your teens can confidently say like Lucy said to me, they are indeed; T—Truthful, E—Empathetic, A—Authentic, C—Caring, H—Helpful, E—Encouraging, R—Role Model. This time they are asking you to add truthfulness, trust and support.

The dictionary refers to a coach as a person who pushes someone to achieve more and supports them when they are struggling. Coaches are people who have the power to influence and impact us positively. They have self-confidence and are willing to help. We must help our teenagers see that we are confident in what we have deposited in them, and can trust them to do well in life on their own with minimal or zero supervision from us. It's okay to also let them know that we are always available to support and help them.

As trees or plants, our teenagers are about to bear the fruits of the seeds we have planted in them. When plants are about to bear fruits, they go through a process. We must approach them with care (respect), so we don't interrupt the process of the flowering and fruit bearing. Parents must understand that becoming your teenager's life coach at this time of their life requires a lot of patience in your approach. You must approach them with more respect, because they are not so little anymore. They want and need to be respected. This is the stage where your negotiation skill becomes your superpower!

These are some of the things every teenager expects from you as their life coach:

- They desire and expect you to respect them because they are growing and discovering themselves.

- They expect you to respect their decisions and trust them to make the right decisions with what you thought them as little children.

- They expect you to respect their boundaries because they are beginning to discover their boundaries too.

- They expect you to be confident in what you have taught them and also trust that they will not fail you.

- They expect your undivided attention when they come to you for help and support; failure to do this may cause them to walk away or shut down.

- They expect you to ask them questions out of love and genuine concern and not out of distrust and fear.

- They expect you to support and help them navigate through life with your guidance, trust, and help.

- They expect you to set your own boundaries and to firmly stick to them. If you set curfew time in the family with consequences for breaking it, follow through. This makes teenagers feel safe and loved. *"Mrs. Nene, I wish my parents where a little firmer with me, I would not have ended this way."* A teen said to me at a seminar.

- They do not want you to relinquish your parental authority to them because you want to please them. They need their parents. A teenager once told me, *"All my life, I have always felt overwhelmed because my parents allowed me to become independent too quickly. I was mentally and emotionally drained. I became a victim to many people who took advantage of me because I was looking for someone to guide and support me as I grew."*

A sports coach does not begin to train his team while they are in the field. He trains them before the game, before he sends his team out there to play. Based on what he has taught them, he shows them that he has confidence in them to win the game. He stays visible but at the background so they know he is committed to supporting them throughout the tough game. He knows that their win is also his win, they know this too. Because he knows the rules of the game, he gives them a tough training and is firm with them so they can follow through and win.

Parents must understand that the teenage stage is tough. It is the stage where your child's learning and values are challenged.

This is when they see others express a level of freedom that looks more attractive than theirs, Unfortunately, if they rationalize, and justify the "attractive freedom" they know the bad behavior will lead to a destructive end. Proverbs 14:12 (TPT) *"You can rationalize it all you want and justify the path of error you have chosen, but you'll find out in the end that you took the road to destruction."* However, if you were engaged in their teaching stages, your children would have naturally needed your support now and would have come back to talk with you. When we overlook the teaching stage of a child, we may end up with a difficult teenager.

The coach and the relationship:

The relationship between the team and the coach is built during the stages of teaching and instructing, which then encourages the team to play the game wholeheartedly. During the time of teaching, children connect with you. Please observe how you have embraced them with your Truthfulness, Empathy, Authenticity, Care, Helpfulness and Hopefulness, and Encouragement. Be a role model. Be a good Role Model to them.

When your children become empowered as individuals, they begin to find answers for themselves. They will come with a goal in mind, determining what their success should be. Parents, who by now are now coaches, can only provide insightful perspective while staying committed to the child's goal because their child is now mature and has a sense of what their success is.

Self-discipline is one invaluable skill every teenager needs to develop at this stage of their life because it helps them stays focused to practice all that they have learned throughout their life. Self-discipline will make them stand out, be in control of their time and self, keep them motivated to achieve their goals, overcome negative peer pressure, and deal with procrastination.

As parents journey into this coaching relationship with their children, it is their responsibility to provide structure, boundaries and a space that enables the child to reflect through these seasons. This can be done by, selecting books for your child to read, or watching movies together and having conversations about what they have learned. Ask the Holy Spirit too, He coaches us through life based on the teachings of Jesus Christ. You know, the Bible tells us that He will bring into remembrance all that we have learned. John 14:26 (NKJV) says, *"But the Comforter, which is the Holy Ghost, whom the Father will send in my name, he shall teach you all things, and bring all things to your remembrance, whatsoever I have said unto you."* Parents, on the other hand, reaffirm what true values are, and what actions that are not consistent with these values and set goals.

During the game:

You will notice during the game, players listen for the voice of the coach. As a parent, your voice at this point will be louder than any other person's once your children are in the field of life. We must be very encouraging with our words, the word "encourage is to empower with courage." The Bible puts it this way in Colossian 4:6 (NLV): *"Speak with them in such a way they will want to listen to you. Do not let your talk sound foolish. Know how to give the right answer to anyone."*

When they are in the game of life, they are attentive to the voice of their coach (parent), know this and give sound advice and affirmations because your opinion matters to them. When they come to you for directions, encouragement, and push, let them know that you are proud of them and believe in them.. Ephesians 4:29 (NIV) advises us: *"Do not let any unwholesome talk come out of your mouths, but only what is helpful for building others up according to their needs, that it may benefit those who listen."*

I believe the best person to coach a child is their parent, and coaching is very effective after the teaching and instructing is done. When coaching is done right, edifying and encouraging words are spoken to our children, they develop right skills that enable them to make right decisions and thrive in life while overcoming challenges in confidence. I am not saying your children have stopped learning; no, what I am saying is that at this stage of their lives, you are giving them all it takes to be independent as they follow your lead.

Coaching means to work alongside an individual to support them to achieve or reach their full potentials across all aspects of life. The Bible refers to children as arrows. Psalm 127:4 says, *"Like arrows in the hands of a warrior are children born in one's youth (NIV).* As parents, we are responsible to shape and sharpen the arrow (our children's lives) to hit that target in life. This is what a coach does effectively with words and actions.

We must understand that sharpening an arrow is a gradual method so is coaching our children. It is not a fast-fix method, but it is a gradual method that helps our children develop life skills as they grow. We must understand that children have limited time to spend with us parents so we have to work on the specific goals and objectives that we want our children to attain before they leave. This is not designed to put pressure on them but to make sure we are satisfied that we shaped them for a better future in life at every stage of parenting.

"Coaching is more focused on supporting the present to create a more positive future" (Robbins, 2019). We must support them to achieve those set goals or objectives by putting down structures now; a structure that will support them to hit the target. Here are some of the structures to put in place when your child needs your support:

- Have a conversation with the teenager and ask lots of leading questions. You must bear in mind that teenagers do not like to give you too much information; that is why you need to ask leading questions.
- You must be attentive to identify the problem that needs being solved.
- Find out what their values are, correct any wrong one they may have picked from their peers and help them fix it while finding solutions to the problem that they brought to you to be solved.
- Express how much you trust them to stand by their values.
- Get resources like books or movies that have emphasis on those values discussed, and watch or read it together.
- Have a retrospective session over these conversations and the problem, ask them what they have learned from the situation.

A parent-coach is responsible for supporting their children to succeed mentally, emotionally, socially, and spiritually and in all aspects of life. Therefore, it is important to support them to build life skills that will aid them in their journey.

How to Coach Your Teenager

- You must be a good listener. Listen without judging, listen without interrupting, listen with curiosity, and listen with empathy.

- At this stage of parenting, teenagers want to be respected, trusted, and perceived differently. Talk to them with respect and seek their own opinion on things. This helps parents understand their thought patterns and how to step in to help.
- Patience is key to coaching, connecting, and reaching the hearts of our children. Be patient and avoid being forceful. Always ensure to keep the conversation open.
- Ask open-ended questions to allow more proactive conversations or dialogue. Open-ended question will always help your children to find answers within themselves. When teenagers give you their own solution to their question or problem, they tend to take ownership of solving the problem. Asking questions stimulates critical thinking. An explorative question boosts their confidence, and reassures them that their thoughts and opinions are legitimate.
- Give positive feedback with the aim to encourage and reinforce trust. When we give positive, non-evaluating, helpful, and relevant feedback, we build and create connecting relationship with our teenagers.
- Mentor and ask follow-up questions. Mentoring helps and provides meaningful connections that impact your children as you influence them.

Here Is an Example of a Parent Coaching Their Teenage Daughter

Diana is a fourteen-year-old teenager who is presently dealing with fear and anxiety in school.

She turns to her parents for help and support (coaching) at this time of her life.

Diana and her parents are having a conversation.

Diana: I feel I am having fears and anxiety.

Parents: How do you mean?

Diana: I feel like I am choking. Most times I feel like I want to puke. There are times I feel like I can't even breathe.

Parents: Can you recall at what time of the day you feel that way? (an open-ended question)

Diana: Every time I see James.

Father: Is James in your class?

Diana: Yes.

Parents: Do you know why you feel that way? (Here is an open-ended question asked by her dad)

Diana: Not really...

Mum: Any ideas about why his presence may be eliciting those reactions? (another open-ended question asked by her mum)

Diana: Not really, Mum. But Dad, I think I feel something for him; I keep thinking about him all the time, and when I see him, I feel he is reading my mind.

Mum: What exactly goes through your mind when you see him? (open-ended question by her mum with an aim of wanting her to be specific)

Diana: I feel I am liking with him.

Parents 2: It's not bad to feel something for him; it's natural, but there is something uneasy within you. What do you think it is?

Diana: Yes, I think it is the fact I am not supposed to be feeling that way toward him now.

Parents 2: I know exactly what you mean. Sometimes we can't stop the emotions from creeping up on us, but we can control how we express them. What do you think you need to do? (Another open-ended question).

Note: At this point we see Diana feeling more relaxed, she thinking about her responses. She is able to name the emotions and expressing herself. He parents continue with the open-ended questions….

Diana: Very true, I feel I think it guilt. I kept feeling like I was doing something wrong or bad.

Parent 1: So how do you think you can handle this now, so you stop feeling guilty? What you feel about him is not wrong, but I think it's the timing that is off. What do you think?

Diana: I will have to deal with my emotions by reminding myself of what I have been taught concerning emotions, friendship, and relationships.

Parents 2: That is awesome! Can you remember the things you were taught?

Diana: Yes, I have power over my emotions. My emotions do not have the driver seat, I do. An intimate relationship between a man and woman is good, but it's for an appointed time, and this is not the time. According to 1 Corinthians 6:18–20, the Bible teaches, *"Flee from sexual immorality. All other sins a person commits are outside the body, but whoever sins sexually, sins against their own body. Do you not know that your bodies are temples of the Holy Spirit, who is in you, whom you have received from God? You are not your own; you were bought at a price. Therefore honor God with your bodies."*

- I am to flee, (stop and control my emotions) from the temptation because the temptation will surely come.
- The sin of fornication (which is sex between two unmarried people) traps. It leads to so many hurts, pains, and regrets. I am bought with a price. I am too precious to God. God does not want that for me.
- My body is the temple of the Holy Spirit; it's not mine but His, and He is in me, so I must honor God with my body.
- I am beautiful, and my beauty is still unfolding and will be used to His glory.

Note: We see Diana, taking responsibility of her thoughts and decisions. She remembers what she has been taught and now puts them to action by owning them and taking responsibility.

Parents: Awesome! Glad you could remember all these. Keep confessing it and reminding yourself and we'll see how it goes. How do you feel now?

Diana: Thanks, Mum and Dad, I feel a lot better and safe to talk about this with you. I will sure let you know how it goes.

A few weeks later, Diana walked into the house all full of smiles. Dad asked across the room, "How is the crush going?"

Diana responding with a smile, "No crush, Dad; it's all gone. We are good friends now. I lost all fear and anxiety the moment I started reminding myself of my values and who I am."

Parents: Awesome!

Diana: All the guilt faded away, and I felt a lot better, and now I feel so great.

Diana: Thank you, Dad and Mum, for creating a safe place for me to talk to you and making me take responsibility for my actions.

"You are welcome, dear, we are always here for you" (her parents said from the other side of the sitting room).

This is what parents are to do with their children while coaching them through challenges of life.

Here are some more benefits of coaching your teens

- Coaching your teenager builds a bond between the both of you for life.

- Coaching your teenager well brings a balance in life between winning and failure, makes them understand that winning is not all that makes one happy, and failure also has its lessons built within it.

- Coaching your teenager helps them take responsibility and makes them own their own experiences

- Coaching empowers us and our teenager to shape and build good habits. (As we build patience with them, we empower them to be more confident.)

- Coaching teenagers makes them see life as a journey and makes them become more self-reliant.

- Coaching brings emotional support to teenagers. They are able to achieve more and become satisfied in life.

- Coaching empowers teenagers to become more accountable for their actions and commitments.

- Coaching will help your children develop and master great life skills. Skills like; effective communication, trust, self-discipline, time management, setting boundaries, respecting other, problem solving and more in the life of a teenager

- Coaching makes teenagers know that they are never alone in life and eases them into working more productively with others.

- Coaching builds trust between you and your teenager opens the channel for effective communication

- Coaching will reduce negative behavior from your teenager

- Coaching your teenagers in a safe psychological environment, where respect, trust, open communication with God centeredness makes them mentally, emotionally, socially and spiritually healthy.

- Coaching makes your teenager honor you.

Here in John 14:26 (NKJV), we read about a phenomenal Person of the Godhead, the Holy Spirit, who is our Teacher, Instructor, and our Helper: *"But the Helper, the Holy Spirit, whom the Father will send in My name, He will teach you all things, and bring to your remembrance all things that I said to you."*

He never judges us but rather judges the world of sin as He reminds us of the standards and values of the kingdom. John 14:8–11 (NKJV) says:

> *And when He has come, He will convict the world of sin, and of righteousness, and of judgment: 9of sin, because they do not believe in Me; 10of righteousness, because I go to My Father and you see Me no more; 11of judgment, because the ruler of this world is judged.*

He leads us into all truth as He guides us. John 14:13 says, *"However, when He, the Spirit of truth, has come, He will guide you into all truth."*

Jesus Christ taught us, He instructed us, and finally He sent the Holy Spirit to coach us.

The Holy Spirit reveals God's mind to us, which is God's perspective to life that leads to success.

I would like to encourage you to always know that, despite your weaknesses, failures and mistakes you are the perfect parent, chosen by God to carry out this assignment of parenting, and His grace is made available as you partner and depend on Him. The Holy Spirit has been sent to coach you through this journey of parenting, reminding you of all that you have learnt. Your labor of love over your children will bear fruits that will remain for generations because parenting is a tree that springs forth with new branches.

> *Ye have not chosen me, but I have chosen you, and ordained you, that ye should go and bring forth fruit, and that your fruit should remain: that whatsoever ye shall ask of the Father in my name, he may give it you."* (John 15:16)

References

1. "Marshall McLuhan Quotes" Brain quote accessed Nov 4, 2022, https://www.brainyquote.com/quotes/marshall_mcluhan_130603

2. "Mahatma Gandhi Quotes" Brain quote accessed Nov 4, 2022, https://www.brainyquote.com/quotes/mahatma_gandhi_133995

3. "Phil Collins Quotes" Goodreads quote accessed Nov 4, 2002 https://www.goodreads.com/quotes/32942-in-learning-you-will-teach-and-in-teaching-you-will

4. "John F. Kennedy Quotes" Brain quote accessed Nov 4, 2022, https://www.brainyquote.com/quotes/john_f_kennedy_130752

5. "Jeannette Walls Quotes" 1000 quotes project accessed Nov4, 2022, *https://1000quotesproject.wordpress.com/2017/05/03/teaching-is-a-calling-too-and-ive-always-thought-that-teachers-in-their-way-are-holy-angels-leading-their-flocks-out-of-darkness/*

6. "Dr. Brene Brown Quotes" YouTube accessed Nov 4, 2022. https://www.youtube.com/watch?v=1Evwgu369Jw

7. "D. C. Tosteson Quotes" Teach with Mrst accessed August 18, 2022 https://www.teachwithmrst.com/post/teachers-as-role-models

8. "Martin Luther King Jr. Quotes" Slide play accessed, Nov 4, 2022 https://slideplayer.com/slide/9951149/

9. "Carl W. Buechner Quotes" Quote investigator accessed, Nov 4, 2022 https://quoteinvestigator.com/2014/04/06/they-feel/

10. "Itzhak Perlman Quotes" Quote fancy accessed, Nov 4, 2022, *https://quotefancy.com/quote/1363620/Itzhak-Perlman-Never-miss-an-opportunity-to-teach-when-you-teach-others-you-teach*

11. "YMCA research poll Quotes" NY post accessed, Nov 4, 2022, https://nypost.com/2018/12/18/these-are-the-top-life-lessons-parents-hope-to-teach-their-kids/

12. "Chuck Swindoll Quotes" Brain quotes accessed, Nov 4, 2022, https://www.brainyquote.com/quotes/charles_r_swindoll_106981

13. "Dwight L. Moody Quotes" AZquotes accessed Nov 4, 2022, https://www.azquotes.com/quote/545590

14. "Mahatma Gandhi Quotes" The Quotations page accessed, Nov 4, 2022, http://www.quotationspage.com/quote/36464.html

15. "*Steve* Jobs Quotes" Brain quotes accessed, Nov 4, 2022, https://www.brainyquote.com/quotes/steve_jobs_416877

16. "Napoleon Hill Quotes" Good read accessed, Nov 4, 2022 https://www.goodreads.com/quotes/1344870-remember-that-your-real-wealth-can-be-measured-not-by

17. "Robert Greene, Mastery Quotes" Good read accessed Nov 4, 2022, https://www.goodreads.com/quotes/740113-the-future-belongs-to-those-who-learn-more-skills-and

18. "Cristina Imre Quotes" Good read accessed Nov 4, 2022, https://www.goodreads.com/author/quotes/8628090.Cristina_Imre#:~:text=%E2%80%9CPeople%20skills%20in%20leadership%20are%20not%20negotiable.%E2%80%9D&tex-

References

t=%E2%80%9CFrequent%20action%20increases%20predictability.%E2%80%9D&text=%E2%80%9CThe%20only%20comparison%20for%20you,only%20person%20you%20should%20outperform.%E2%80%9D

19. "Meagan Francis Quotes" Pinterest accessed, Nov 4, 2022 https://www.pinterest.com/pin/368169338286991293/

20. "Winston Churchill Quotes" Forbes quotes accessed, Nov 4, 2022, https://www.forbes.com/quotes/10341/

21. "Abhishek Ratna Quotes" Bukrate accessed, Nov 4, 2022, https://bukrate.com/quote/1685692

22. "Dieter F. Uchtdorf Quotes" Quote Catalog accessed, Nov 4, 2022, https://quotecatalog.com/quote/dieter-f-uchtdorf-its-your-rea-zpWMkg1/

23. "Eric Thomas Quotes" Quote Fancy accessed Nov 4, 2022, https://quotefancy.com/quote/1579020/Eric-Thomas-I-learned-that-a-real-friendship-is-not-about-what-you-can-get-but-what-you

24. "Marcus Tullius Cicero Quotes" Todayinsci accessed, Nov 7, 2022, https://todayinsci.com/C/Cicero_Marcus/CiceroMarcus-MindFruitQuote800px.htm

25. "Solomon Quotes" *Quote Fancy accessed, Nov 7, 2022,* https://quotefancy.com/quote/1708322/Solomon-A-wise-person-will-listen-and-take-in-more-instruction

26. "Ric Charlesworth Quotes" *Quotes Fancy accessed, Nov 7, 2022* https://quotefancy.com/quote/1638215/Ric-Charlesworth-The-interesting-thing-about-coaching-is-that-you-have-to-trouble-the

27. "Brian Cagneey Quotes" Flash Point accessed, Nov 7, 2022, https://www.flashpointleadership.com/blog/make-time-for-coaching-and-development

28. "Elaine MacDonald Quotes" Brainy Quote accessed, Nov 7, 2022, https://www.brainyquote.com/quotes/elaine_macdonald_293166
29. "Duvall 1957 Family Quote". Iastate Pressbooks accessed, Nov 7, 2022, https://iastate.pressbooks.pub/parentingfamilydiversity/chapter/the-family-life-cycle-theory/

CPSIA information can be obtained
at www.ICGtesting.com
Printed in the USA
BVHW071519130123
656260BV00007B/541